"Ray Stedman made a ntial where I did not. H
more than I was. He r
out my 'blind spots.' I
He made me want to be a mentor myself. As a result of being
mentored by Ray, I learned the value of being vulnerable, open,
unguarded, and honest—a person of authenticity."

—CHARLES R. SWINDOLL
Best-selling author, speaker, and Bible teacher

"I loved Ray Stedman! What I remember most about Ray Stedman: Ray was humorous. He was filled with the joy of the Lord.
Ray was a real man. He was a man's man in every way. Ray was
authentic. He loved you enough to firmly rebuke you when
needed. His practical application of Scripture quickly shook
your conscience. . . . Ray lived out the resurrected indwelling
life of a Christian unlike any man I have known, and he taught
us well."

—LUIS PALAU
International evangelist

"I am a rich man for having had a companionship with Ray
Stedman. Ray was unique, impossible to encapsulate in words,
but he was a man through whom God's Spirit brought light
to darkened minds, a man totally devoted to serving our Savior, and solid proof that it is not the man but the message that
makes the difference."

—HOWARD G. HENDRICKS
Noted theologian, author, and Christian mentor

Also by Ray C. Stedman

Adventuring through the Bible

Authentic Christianity

Body Life

The Fight of Faith

For Such a Time as This

Friend of God

God's Blueprint for Success

God's Final Word

God's Loving Word

God's Unfinished Book

Hope in a Chaotic World

Is This All There Is to Life?

Let God Be God

Letters to a Troubled Church

A Nation in Crisis

On the Way to the Future

Our Riches in Christ

The Power of His Presence

Psalms: Folk Songs of Faith

Reason to Rejoice

Spiritual Warfare

Talking with My Father

The Way to Wholeness

What on Earth Is Happening?

About Ray C. Stedman

Portrait of Integrity: The Life of Ray C. Stedman
by Mark Mitchell

Ray Stedman
on Leadership

40
LESSONS
from an
INFLUENTIAL
MENTOR

Ray C. Stedman *with* Jim Denney

Discovery House.
from Our Daily Bread Ministries

Ray Stedman on Leadership
© 2019 by Elaine Stedman
All rights reserved.

Discovery House is affiliated with Our Daily Bread Ministries,
Grand Rapids, Michigan.

Requests for permission to quote from this book should be directed
to: Permissions Department, Discovery House, PO Box 3566, Grand
Rapids, MI 49501, or contact us by email at permissionsdept@dhp.org.

Foreword adapted from "The Enduring Value of a Mentor" by Charles
R. Swindoll. Copyright © 2013 by Charles R. Swindoll, Inc. All rights
reserved worldwide. Used by permission. insight.org.

All Scripture quotations, unless otherwise indicated, are taken from the
Holy Bible, New International Version®, NIV®. Copyright © 1973,
1978, 1984, 2011 by Biblica, Inc.® Used by permission of Zondervan.
All rights reserved worldwide. zondervan.com. The "NIV" and "New
International Version" are trademarks registered in the United States
Patent and Trademark Office by Biblica, Inc.®

Scripture quotations marked MEV are taken from the Modern English
Version. Copyright © 2014 by Military Bible Association. Used by
permission. All rights reserved.

Interior design by Beth Shagene

ISBN: 978-1-62707-944-0

Printed in the United States of America

First printing in 2019

Contents

The Enduring Influence
of Ray Stedman

THERE WE SAT, A CLUSTER OF SIX. A STUBBY ORANGE candle burned at the center of our table, flickering shadows across our faces. One spoke; five listened. Every question was handled with such grace, such ease—each answer drawn from deep wells of wisdom, shaped by tough decisions, nurtured by time. And pain. And mistakes and mistreatment. Honed by tests, risks, heartbreaks, and failures. Decades in the same crucible had made this man's counsel invaluable.

His age? Seventy-two. He had weathered it all—all the flack and delights of a flock. He had outlasted all the fads and gimmicks of gullible and greedy generations. He had known the ecstasy of seeing lives revolutionized, as well as the agony of lives ruined and the heartbreaking monotony of lives unchanged. He had paid his dues—with the scars to prove it.

We sat for more than three hours hearing his stories, pondering his principles, and probing his conclusions. The evening was punctuated with periodic outbursts of laughter followed by protracted periods of quiet talk. As I participated, suddenly, I was twenty-six again—a young seminarian and pastoral intern existing in a no-man's-land between a heart full of desire and a head full of dreams. Long on theological theories but short on practical experience, I had answers to questions no one was asking and a lack of understanding about the things that really mattered. I was in great need of being mentored.

In flashbacks, I saw myself in the same room with this man thirty years earlier, drinking at the same well, soaking up the same spirit. Thirty years ago, Ray Stedman had been my model; now he had become my mentor.

I've discovered that when people are young and gifted, the most common tendency is for them to drift toward arrogance and, sometimes, raw conceit. Almost without exception, when I detect conceit in individuals, I think to myself, *They haven't been mentored.* Mentoring can inhibit drifting. I've never met a self-important, arrogant individual who has been well mentored. Arrogance doesn't survive mentoring. A mentor points out blind spots and reproves you when you need to be confronted about your pride. A mentor won't back off. A mentor relentlessly presses for excellence. A mentor cares about your character.

That was Ray. Thoroughly human and absolutely authentic, he had emerged a well-worn vessel of honor fit for the Master's use. And that night around that little orange candle, I found myself profoundly grateful that Ray's shadow had crossed my life.

In Paul's final letter to Timothy, we read these words: "The things which you have heard from me in the presence of many witnesses, entrust these to faithful men who will be able to teach others also" (2 Timothy 2:2). *Entrust* literally means to hand over "something to someone . . . for safekeeping." I like that image. We invest the truth like a trust in the lives of others. We have a valuable message we pass along to others. Paul the apostle entrusted his heart, soul, truths, confrontations, encouragements, affirmations—his very life—to Timothy. That's what Ray did for me.

Ray Stedman made a major difference in my life. He saw potential where I did not. He encouraged me to become someone more than I was. He reproved and corrected me. He pointed out my "blind spots." He modeled what I longed to become. He made me want to be a mentor myself. As a result of being mentored by Ray, I learned the value of being vulnerable, open, unguarded, and honest—a person of authenticity.

I'll never forget that evening with Ray Stedman. As I said goodbye that night, I walked a little slower. I thought about the things Ray had taught me without directly instructing me, the courage he had given me without deliberately exhorting me. I found myself wanting to run back to his car and tell him again how much I loved and admired him—my mentor. I wish I had done that.

And as I stood there alone in the cold night air, I suddenly realized what I wanted to be when I grew up.

—CHARLES R. SWINDOLL

Charles R. Swindoll has devoted his life to the accurate, practical teaching and application of God's Word. Since 1998, he has served as the senior pastor-teacher of Stonebriar Community Church in Frisco, Texas, but Chuck's listening audience extends beyond a local church body. As a leading program in Christian broadcasting since 1979, Insight for Living *airs around the world. Chuck's leadership as president and now chancellor of Dallas Theological Seminary has helped prepare and equip a new generation for ministry.*

INTRODUCTION

About Ray Stedman

RAY STEDMAN (1917–1992) SERVED AS PASTOR OF THE
Peninsula Bible Church in Palo Alto, California, from 1950 to
1990, where he was known and loved as a man of outstanding
Bible knowledge, Christian integrity, warmth, and humility.

Born in Temvik, North Dakota, Ray spent the bulk of his
childhood living in the rugged landscape of Montana. When he
was a small child, his mother became ill and his father, a railroad
man, abandoned the family. Ray grew up on his aunt's Montana
farm from the time he was six. At age eleven, he gave his life to
Jesus during a Methodist revival meeting.

As a young man, Ray moved around the country trying
different jobs, working in Chicago, Denver, Hawaii, and else-
where. He enlisted in the Navy during World War II, where he
often led Bible studies for civilians and Navy personnel—and
even preached on local radio in Hawaii. At the close of the war,
Ray married his wife, Elaine, in Honolulu. They returned to the
mainland in 1946, where Ray began attending Dallas Theological Seminary. After two summers interning under Dr. J. Vernon
McGee, he traveled for several months with Dr. H.A. Ironside,
pastor of Moody Church in Chicago.

In 1950, a fledgling church in Palo Alto, California contacted John Walvoord, president of Dallas Theological Seminary, in search of its first pastor. Dr. Walvoord recommended a seminary student who was just about to graduate: Ray Stedman. Peninsula Bible Fellowship hired Ray as "Executive Director, without a guaranteed salary," and only later realized they'd brought in Ray without ever hearing him preach! But he began his ministry there in September of 1950 anyway, and stayed for nearly forty years before retiring in April of 1990.

Peninsula Bible Fellowship later became Peninsula Bible Church, and during his years there, Ray Stedman invested his life in teaching the Bible, mentoring others, and writing some of the now-classic Christian works of the twentieth century, including *Body Life*, *Authentic Christianity*, *Adventuring through the Bible*, and many expository studies of Scripture.

Along the way, Ray became mentor to some of the most influential leaders of our time: Chuck Swindoll, Luis Palau, Howard Hendricks, and many more. His passion for Christ, wisdom with Scripture, and lifestyle of joy have influenced literally millions of people worldwide.

Ray Stedman joined Jesus in heaven on October 7, 1992.

1

The Servant Who Leads

Mark 8

DR. JAMES ALLAN FRANCIS (1864–1928) ONCE DESCRIBED the life and accomplishments of Jesus of Nazareth in a short essay called "One Solitary Life." He wrote:

> He worked in a carpenter shop until He was thirty, and then for three years He was an itinerant preacher. He never wrote a book. He never held an office. He never owned a home. He never had a family. He never went to college. He never put his foot inside a big city. He never traveled two hundred miles from the place where He was born. He never did one of the things that usually accompany greatness. . . .
>
> Nineteen wide centuries have come and gone and today He is the centerpiece of the human race and the leader of the column of progress . . . All the kings that ever reigned, put together, have not affected the life of man upon this earth as powerfully as has that One Solitary Life.[1]

Who was the greatest leader in human history? Jesus of Nazareth. He founded a global spiritual movement by investing three years of his life in twelve unexceptional men. He taught them, mentored them—and then He left them. Today the spiritual movement Jesus founded—the church—has endured for some 2,000 years and numbers more than 2.5 billion followers.

If a leader can start with nothing and create a grassroots movement that endures and grows for more than twenty centuries—that's a leader worth learning from. How did He get people to listen to Him? How did He get people to follow Him? Did He promise them a life of prosperity and ease? Did He promise them power and position?

No. He called people to a life of adversity and self-sacrifice, of serving and suffering. He gathered a crowd of people together and told them, "Whoever wants to be my disciple must deny themselves and take up their cross and follow me. For whoever wants to save their life will lose it, but whoever loses their life for me and for the gospel will save it" (Mark 8:34–35).

This is our Lord's outline of the process of discipleship. Here, He tells us what it means to be His disciple. To follow Jesus, you have to give up the right to run your own life. You must submit to His lordship and leadership. If you're not willing to deny yourself, you can't be His disciple.

What does Jesus mean when He says we must deny ourselves? He doesn't mean we must hate ourselves or neglect our basic physical needs, such as food, water, and sleep. When Jesus says we are to deny ourselves, the original Greek text uses the word *aparneomai*, which means "to disavow any connection with something." It's the same Greek word used to describe what Peter did and said when he denied Jesus three times during the Lord's trial, the night before the crucifixion. Peter denied having any connection to the Lord—and Jesus tells us we are to deny having any connection to ourselves, any right to ourselves, any say over our own lives.

Jesus is making a radical statement that strikes at the heart of our being. If there is one thing that we human beings value and protect above all else, it's our right to self-determination. The moment we sense that someone is infringing on our right to make our own decisions and live our own lives, we say, "You can't boss me around! You can't tell me what to do!" Yet our right to self-determination is *exactly* what Jesus says we *must* give up.

Carved on the wall of the auditorium of Peninsula Bible Church, where I served as pastor for four decades, are these words from the apostle Paul's first letter to the Christians in Corinth (6:19–20): "You are not your own; you are bought with a price." If you are going to follow Jesus, you must surrender all rights to Him. He is now the Lord of your life—you are not. He makes the great and momentous decisions of your life—and you say, "Yes, Lord." He is the Master.

As disciples, we follow Him and pattern our leadership style after His. We share the gospel He taught us. We serve others as He served. We love our enemies, pray for those who hurt us, and forgive those who offend us. We live humbly and selflessly as He did. We oppose evil and hypocrisy as He did—especially the evil and hypocrisy we find in ourselves. We gather a few people around us and invest our lives in them, as He invested in the Twelve.

Jesus is the source of our leadership ministry. He breaks the bread that feeds the multitude, but He sends us, His disciples, to distribute that bread to the needy and hungry. We must continually look to Him for the pattern and for the power.

He is not interested in making us into slightly improved versions of our old selves. If we accept the challenge of being His disciples, He is going to shatter us and rebuild us into brand-new people. He is reshaping us to the core of our being. He is remaking us in His own image.

Jesus is the Servant who leads. He led and served the Twelve, and through them He changed the course of history. And we are learning to lead as He led. What does He want to achieve through you and me?

"So Christ himself gave the apostles, the prophets, the evangelists, the pastors and teachers, to equip his people for works of service, so that the body of Christ may be built up until we all reach unity in the faith and in the knowledge of the Son of God and become mature, attaining to the whole measure of the fullness of Christ." —EPHESIANS 4:11–13

FOR FURTHER REFLECTION:

1. In what ways do you see Jesus as a role model for leaders? Make a list.

2. In what ways is Jesus a role model for the way *you* lead? Describe it.

3. How has Jesus's example helped you make a leadership decision in the past month? How will His example help you in the next month?

4. What prevents you from leading like Jesus? What can you do about that tomorrow?

2

The Leader Who Serves

Mark 8

I ONCE PICKED UP A YOUNG HITCHHIKER. WE CHATTED AS we drove, and at one point he told me, "My uncle died a millionaire." I said, "No, he didn't. Your uncle died with nothing." The young man looked surprised and said, "Why do you say that? You don't know my uncle. He had millions!" I said, "Who has those millions now?" The young man nodded slowly. "Oh, I see what you mean."

Nobody dies a millionaire. We all die with nothing.

But Jesus shows us a way to be rich in this life, and in the life to come. How do we achieve these riches of Jesus? Let's look again at his message to the crowd in Mark 8:

"Whoever wants to be my disciple must deny themselves and take up their cross and follow me. For whoever wants to save their life will lose it, but whoever loses their life for me and for the gospel will save it" (Mark 8:34–35).

When the people first heard Jesus speak these words, they must have wondered, *What does He mean—"take up your cross"?* They had seen the Roman instrument of execution before—but they didn't know that Jesus Himself was about to be nailed to the cross and tortured to death. Jesus knew what the cross would mean, but the people who heard Him did not.

Some people mistakenly think that a hardship they're enduring—a troublesome neighbor, a difficult boss, a financial difficulty, a physical handicap—is the "cross" they must bear. But that's not what Jesus meant. When He spoke of the cross, He was referring to the shame and humiliation of the cross. Crucifixion was a criminal's death, a demeaning and degrading form of death. When Jesus said we are to take up our cross, He was telling us that we are to welcome the shame and humiliation of the cross. The cross is the place where we put pride to death.

Do you resent it when people insult you, embarrass you, make fun of you, yell at you, cut you off on the freeway? That's your pride at work. Crucify it. Do you envy what others have? Do you feel you have a right to a certain standard of living, a promotion at work, a bigger home, a better car? That's your pride showing. Crucify it. It's not wrong to have these things, but everything we have is a gift of God's grace, not a right or an entitlement. To feel entitled to such things is pride. Crucify pride.

After "take up your cross," the Lord says, "and follow Me." To follow Jesus is to obey Him and walk in His footsteps, patterning our lives, our words, our actions after His. Disobedience is the way of this world. Obedience is the essence of following Jesus. Yes, we struggle and fail. But when we stray from the path of obedience, we pick ourselves up, confess our sins, and get back on the path of following Him.

This is what it means to be a disciple: Deny yourself, take up your cross, and follow Him. In the original Greek, these steps are stated in the present continuous tense. We are to continuously deny ourselves, continuously take up our cross, continually and persistently follow Him. This is not a once-and-for-all decision, but a program for a lifetime, and it must be repeated over and over.

Jesus gives us a new motive for living: "For whoever wants to save their life will lose it, but whoever loses their life for me and for the gospel will save it." Who doesn't desperately want to save his or her life? Who doesn't want this life to matter? Who doesn't want a life that is full, rich, and worth living? We all want that. And Jesus tells us, "If this is what you want, I'll tell you how to acquire it: lose your life for Me and for the gospel, and you will save your life."

In other words, deny yourself, disavow yourself, and you will find a life worth living. Hold on to your desire for comfort, entitlement, status, power, praise, money, fame, or any other worldly goal—and you will ultimately lose everything. You'll die having wasted your one and only life.

If we live for ourselves, we will lose our lives. If we lose our lives for Him, we will save our lives for all eternity. But equally important, we will save our lives in the here and now.

If we lose our lives for Him, we will find contentment and satisfaction, an inner peace, and the conviction that we are living for a worthwhile cause. Though you may forego some of the momentary pleasures, power, and status symbols others have, your life will be rich, rewarding, and meaningful.

Finally, Jesus poses this all-important question to you and me: "What good is it for someone to gain the whole world, yet forfeit their soul?" (Mark 8:36).

The most powerful leader of the Middle Ages was Charlemagne (742–814), the king of the Frankish Empire. After an extended hunting trip, he contracted pneumonia and died on January 28, 814. Two centuries after his death, a nobleman named Otho of Lomello claimed he broke into the tomb of Charlemagne. Though some historians doubt his account, Otho claimed he found Charlemagne's body seated upon a throne, wrapped in robes with a crown on his head, appearing to be merely asleep. On his lap was a Bible opened to the Gospel of Mark. It's said that Charlemagne's index finger pointed to Mark 8:36, as if the king, even in death, was contemplating the question: What good will it do to gain the whole world yet forfeit your soul?

To be a leader of meaning and purpose, deny yourself, take up your cross, and follow Jesus.

"In your relationships with one another, have the same mindset as Christ Jesus: Who, being in very nature God, did not consider equality with God something to be used to his own advantage; rather, he made himself nothing by taking the very nature of a servant, being made in human likeness. And being found in appearance as a man, he humbled himself by becoming obedient to death—even death on a cross."

—PHILIPPIANS 2:5–8

FOR FURTHER REFLECTION:

1. What motivates you to lead? Explain.

2. What does it really mean for you, as a leader, to "take up your cross" and follow Jesus? Describe it in bullet points.

3. Jesus said we are to take up our cross, implying we are to welcome the shame and humiliation that comes with it. How does that play out in your role as a leader?

4. What are five steps you can take this week to better live out Ray Stedman's advice on servant leadership?

3

The Greatest Leader

Mark 9

EVANGELIST ALAN REDPATH ONCE SAID, "PRIDE IS THE idolatrous worship of ourselves, and that is the national religion of hell."[1] Pride is a deadly pitfall of leadership. When Jesus discipled the Twelve, He continually confronted their pride.

In Mark 9, we catch a glimpse into the mentoring ministry Jesus had with His disciples. Mark writes:

> They left that place and passed through Galilee. Jesus did not want anyone to know where they were, because he was teaching his disciples. He said to them, "The Son of Man is going to be delivered into the hands of men. They will kill him, and after three days he will rise." But they did not understand what he meant and were afraid to ask him about it. (Mark 9:30–32)

The Lord had a public teaching ministry to the crowds, but He also had a private mentoring ministry among the Twelve. As they made their way through Galilee, toward Capernaum, Jesus took the back roads, avoiding the crowds so He could spend vital time teaching the disciples. His primary goal was to prepare the Twelve for the leadership roles they would have after His departure. He was intent on preparing them for ministry. That was His plan for building His church.

Jesus and the disciples paused beside the road, and He talked to them about coming events. He told them He would be betrayed and executed—and after three days, He would rise from the dead. The disciples didn't understand what Jesus meant—and were afraid to ask. They weren't afraid that Jesus would rebuke them for asking questions. No, they feared what His answer might be. They were in denial, hoping Jesus didn't really mean what He was saying. It's common for people to deal with unpleasant news by saying, "Let's not talk about it, let's not even think about it."

One of the Twelve was Judas Iscariot, who would later betray Jesus. Did Judas know the role he would play in the betrayal and death of Jesus? Was he already planning to sell Jesus out for thirty pieces of silver? We don't know. But Judas may have feared that Jesus knew what he was planning.

Jesus knew that, one day, the disciples would look back and understand that He had been strengthening them for the challenges ahead. Next Mark writes:

> They came to Capernaum. When he was in the house, he asked them, "What were you arguing about on the road?" But they kept quiet because on the way they had argued about who was the greatest
>
> Sitting down, Jesus called the Twelve and said, "Anyone who wants to be first must be the very last, and the servant of all."
>
> He took a little child whom he placed among them. Taking the child in his arms, he said to them, "Whoever welcomes one of these little children in my name welcomes

me; and whoever welcomes me does not welcome me but the one who sent me." (Mark 9:33–37)

When they reached Capernaum, Jesus asked the disciples about their argument on the road. They responded with embarrassed silence. They realized that their pride, envy, and pettiness had been laid bare before the Master—after all He had taught them about denying themselves, taking up their cross, and following Him!

So Jesus gathered the Twelve around Him and taught them about one of the great dangers of leadership—the snare of prideful ambition. "Anyone who wants to be first," He told them, "must be the very last, and the servant of all."

Jesus did not rebuke them for being ambitious. He didn't condemn them for wanting to be the greatest. God has built into every human heart a desire to excel, to succeed, to achieve. That's not a sinful desire—that's a godly desire. It becomes sinful when it becomes prideful, when we seek to be admired, praised, and glorified for our accomplishments. It becomes sinful when we use our accomplishments to lord it over others. But the desire to accomplish great things is not an ungodly desire.

He revealed to the disciples the secret for preventing godly ambitions from becoming satanic pride and arrogance. The secret is this: If you want to be truly great, you must give up the ambition to be first. Be willing to be last. Give up the desire to be served. Become the servant of all. That is the key to godly greatness.

Jesus was saying that there are two kinds of greatness, two kinds of ambition. One is the fleshly ambition to be admired and applauded by the world. The other is the spiritual ambition to be approved and commended by God. These two ambitions are as different as night and day.

God doesn't measure greatness the way we do. Those who are great in God's eyes are those who ask, "How many people have I served today? How many lives have I influenced for God? How many children have I blessed? How many feet have I washed?"

Ours is a radical faith. It upends our thinking. It revolutionizes our lives. It saws across the grain of the wisdom of this world. That's why, the more mature we grow as Christians, the more we act against our natural instincts and inclinations. We learn that the leadership style of Jesus runs counter to the power-obsessed leadership model of this dying world.

To drive this leadership lesson home, Jesus called a child to Him, wrapped the child in His loving arms, and said, "Whoever welcomes one of these little children in my name welcomes me; and whoever welcomes me does not welcome me but the one who sent me." What a memorable way for Jesus to make the point.

Whatever we do for a child, we do unto the Lord. A child can't repay your kindness or help you in any way. There's no benefit for you in helping a child. Your motivation in welcoming that child is serving Jesus the Master—and when you serve Jesus, you serve God the Father.

Is Jesus only concerned with children? No. The child in His arms symbolizes all human souls who are needy, helpless, defenseless—people who need our help and can never repay us. That child stands for the poor, the displaced, the marginalized. That child stands for those who are impoverished, oppressed, in prison, or in a hospital. We who have been blessed with health and resources and the good news of Jesus Christ must be the arms of Jesus, wrapped lovingly around the least and the last and the lost, meeting their needs in the name of the Master. A cup of cold water, offered in Jesus's name, will never lose its reward.

I opened with a quote by Alan Redpath. I close with a story

he told of a lady who had a plaque on the wall next to her kitchen sink. The plaque read, "Divine service is conducted here three times daily." The kitchen sink is where she peeled potatoes, rinsed chicken parts, and washed dishes. The work she did at that sink didn't make her famous or wealthy or powerful in the eyes of the world. But three times a day, she did divine service in the name of Jesus at that sink. I have no doubt that the Lord was well pleased with her service.

The greatest leader is the servant of all.

"Do nothing out of selfish ambition or vain conceit. Rather, in humility value others above yourselves, not looking to your own interests but each of you to the interests of the others."
—PHILIPPIANS 2:3–4

FOR FURTHER REFLECTION:

1. How do you balance the competing priorities of public leadership and private mentorship? Draw a map or diagram to visualize it.

2. What are five principles of mentorship you see in Jesus's example of Mark 9:30–37?

3. What is the fearful question you have for Jesus—and why does it make you feel worried? Explain.

4. "Anyone who wants to be first must be the very last, and the servant of all." What changes can you make this week to better follow this truth in the way you lead others?

4

Death of a Leader

Mark 10

I ONCE VISITED THE HOME OF A MAN I HAD BEEN COUNSEL-
ing for several months. When I arrived, I found the front door
standing open. I called his name. No one answered. I went
inside and called out, but the house was silent.

I came to a room and found him dead on the floor. He had
committed suicide.

It was one of the worst shocks of my life to find someone I
had known and prayed with—someone I had tried to help—
dead by his own hand.

There's no subject we can ponder that is more troubling to
the soul than death. This is true whether it is our own death or
the death of someone we care about.

In Mark 10, Jesus and His disciples were on the road to Jerusalem, and Jesus began talking to them about death—His own
fast-approaching death. They were moving into the final week
before the cross. Jesus clearly foresaw all that it would entail, and
He was determined to face what was to come:

> They were on their way up to Jerusalem, with Jesus lead-
> ing the way, and the disciples were astonished, while those

who followed were afraid. Again he took the Twelve aside and told them what was going to happen to him. "We are going up to Jerusalem," he said, "and the Son of Man will be delivered over to the chief priests and the teachers of the law. They will condemn him to death and will hand him over to the Gentiles, who will mock him and spit on him, flog him and kill him. Three days later he will rise." (Mark 10:32–34)

Once again, Jesus told the disciples that He was about to suffer and die—and this time, He provided more details. And again, He also promised His resurrection after three days.

It's significant that Jesus went in the lead, alone, with no one at His side. His band of disciples walked along behind Him—and behind them was the multitude who always waited upon His teaching. Mark tells us that those who followed Jesus "were afraid." Both the disciples and the crowd felt a sense of approaching crisis.

In this prediction of His death, He included details He had never revealed before: the chief priests and teachers of the law were going to hand Him over to the Gentiles. The Roman oppressors were going to mock Him, spit on Him, flog Him, and execute Him. How did Jesus know what was going to happen? He knew the Scriptures—passages like Isaiah 53 and Psalm 22 that predicted the suffering and death of the Messiah.

But even after Jesus told them plainly about His death, the disciples didn't understand—or didn't *want* to understand— what awaited Him. They didn't understand the Old Testament passages about the suffering Messiah. They still expected Jesus to be the triumphant Messiah. With the benefit of hindsight, we understand that the Messiah had to go through the suffering of the cross before He could come into His glory. Because of their lack of understanding, two disciples stepped forward and boldly asked a favor of Jesus:

> Then James and John, the sons of Zebedee, came to him. "Teacher," they said, "we want you to do for us whatever we ask."
> "What do you want me to do for you?" he asked.
> They replied, "Let one of us sit at your right and the other at your left in your glory." (Mark 10:35–37)

Though Jesus spoke of His coming death, James and John were focused on His eventual glory. They asked that Jesus give them each a place at His side. Many Bible teachers have criticized the sons of Zebedee for this request, but I don't believe they were wrong to ask. Jesus gave them every reason to make this request.

Matthew records an earlier conversation Jesus had with the Twelve, when He said, "Truly I tell you, at the renewal of all things, when the Son of Man sits on his glorious throne, you who have followed me will also sit on twelve thrones, judging the twelve tribes of Israel" (Matthew 19:28). By faith, James and John believed that twelve thrones awaited them.

They didn't ask for anything wrong. Jesus said to them that what they wanted was right, but they were going about it the wrong way:

> "You don't know what you are asking," Jesus said. "Can you drink the cup I drink or be baptized with the baptism I am baptized with?"
> "We can," they answered.
> Jesus said to them, "You will drink the cup I drink and be baptized with the baptism I am baptized with, but to sit at my right or left is not for me to grant. These places

belong to those for whom they have been prepared." (Mark 10:38–40)

He said, in effect, "You are asking for a good thing, but you are asking in ignorance. You don't know what you will have to go through to sit next to Me in glory." Jesus knew the price and was ready to pay it. James and John *thought* they knew the price, but they had no idea what lay before them.

Jesus spoke of the cup He would drink and the baptism He would undergo. He would speak of this same cup in His prayer in the Garden of Gethsemane: "Father, if you are willing, take this cup from me; yet not my will, but yours be done" (Luke 22:42).

The cup spoke of the entire spectrum of events that would soon engulf Him—the violent suffering, the emotional and spiritual agony, the rejection, the mocking and scourging, and ultimately death on the cross. Baptism was a common image in Israelite culture; when the Israelites left Egypt they were "baptized into Moses" in the Red Sea (see 1 Corinthians 10:2). The sea opened up, the people walked between walls of water, and they were surrounded by the sea. It was a symbolic picture of passing through death and rising in resurrection.

The Lord said to James and John, in effect, "This is the price of glory. Are you able to pay it?" In their human over-confidence, they said, "We can."

What did Jesus mean when he said that James and John would "drink the cup I drink"? He was saying that they would suffer the reproach and anguish of martyrdom. History records that James was the first of the apostles to be martyred (he was beheaded by Herod, as recorded in Acts 12:2). John was the last of the apostles to die. These two brothers form a "parenthesis of martyrdom." All the other apostles were martyred for their faith between these two brothers.

History doesn't tell us how John died. We do know he was exiled to the island of Patmos because of his testimony for the Lord Jesus. There he suffered for the Lord's sake, and also received the vision that forms the Book of Revelation.

Leadership is the art of accomplishing great things through other people. Jesus started with twelve ordinary men, and through His leadership, He transformed them into the foundation for a global spiritual movement, the church. He taught them and poured His life into them. With the lone exception of Judas the traitor, they all became leaders, living as He lived, teaching as He taught, leading as He led—and finally, dying as He died.

"I want to know Christ—yes, to know the power of his resurrection and participation in his sufferings, becoming like him in his death, and so, somehow, attaining to the resurrection from the dead." —PHILIPPIANS 3:10–11

FOR FURTHER REFLECTION:

1. Why do you think the disciples refused to think about Jesus's coming death, even after He spoke so plainly, and in detail, about the crucifixion?

2. What leadership lessons do you see in the way Jesus tried to prepare His disciples for the very difficult time that was coming? Make a list.

3. How do you keep faith in very difficult times? Write about one specific time.

4. What can you do tomorrow to help strengthen one of your followers who is facing difficulty?

5

Preeminence, Proximity, and Power

Mark 10

I ONCE MET WITH A PASTOR WHO HAD SERVED GOD FOR years but had recently seen his ministry collapse in ruins. It was an embarrassing, humbling experience for this dedicated Christian leader. We sat and talked about his painful experience.

"I prided myself on my faithfulness and dedication to God," he said. "I looked down on people who were not as dedicated as I was. I thought I was being very spiritual and committed, a true servant of God. I told myself that God was fortunate to have me on His team."

Then he told me about the collapse of his ministry. "Now I look back," he said, "and I realize I was only feeding my own ego."

Our human capacity for self-deception has no limits. We think we are serving God out of pure motives and a genuine desire to serve Him—yet all the while, our "service" is driven by selfish pride. It's hard to know exactly what motivated James and John to ask that Jesus give them the two thrones closest to

Him. We know that Jesus didn't rebuke them. He said that what they wanted was right, but they went about it the wrong way:

Let's look at what James and John were asking for. On close examination, we see that their request contained three elements:

First, James and John asked for *preeminence*. They wanted the honor a throne represents. And why shouldn't they want it? That's what Jesus had promised them.

Second, James and John asked for *proximity*. Once the disciples knew that twelve thrones awaited them, they wanted to be closest to the Lord. The twelve had previously argued among themselves about who would be the greatest, and they believed that greatness was measured in their closeness to Jesus. Was it wrong to want to be close to Jesus? I don't think so. Every believer should want to be close to Him.

Third, they wanted *power*. That's what a throne represents. They had already experienced the gift of power from Jesus. The Lord had sent them out with power to preach, heal, raise the dead, and cast out demons. They were only asking for more of what Jesus had already given them.

Jesus didn't rebuke James and John for wanting preeminence, proximity, or power. In fact, to be an effective leader, preeminence, proximity, and power are three qualities you *must* have.

Preeminence is visibility—your people need to see you, hear you, and recognize you as their leader or they will not be able to follow you. Proximity is closeness—you need to be close to God in order to lead your people in a godly way, and your people need to be close to you to be influenced by your godly leadership. Power is influence—you need the power of communication, of persuasion, of authentic godly character. You need the power to inspire and motivate people so they will achieve the goals you set for them.

How did the other disciples respond when James and John

made their request? Mark tells us, "When the ten heard about this, they became indignant with James and John" (Mark 10:41). The conflict among the Twelve gave Jesus a teaching opportunity:

> Jesus called them together and said, "You know that those who are regarded as rulers of the Gentiles lord it over them, and their high officials exercise authority over them. Not so with you. Instead, whoever wants to become great among you must be your servant, and whoever wants to be first must be slave of all. For even the Son of Man did not come to be served, but to serve, and to give his life as a ransom for many." (Mark 10:42–45)

But Jesus swept aside the envy and strife of the Twelve. That's how the world works, He said in effect, but that is not how My church should function. Leaders in the church are not to strive with each other for position and honor. In the Gentile world, leadership is about being the boss. It's about lording it over other people.

Then Jesus said something radical: "Not so with you." The church was not to be run the way the Gentiles ran their power structures. Godly leadership is not about being the boss. It's about being a servant. Whoever would be great, whoever would be a leader, must become the servant and slave of all. When we give ourselves to meet the needs of others, a paradox takes place: we establish authority in the life of the person we serve. They want to respond to our leadership.

Worldly leadership compels and intimidates people into obedience. Godly leadership inspires and attracts people to become enthusiastic, obedient followers. Jesus never browbeat His followers. He loved them and served them, and they loved Him back and wanted to please Him. Jesus sums up His teaching on leadership by offering himself as an example: "For even the Son of Man did not come to be served, but to serve, and to give his life as a ransom for many" (Mark 10:45).

He is the ultimate picture of a leader who serves. He demonstrates godly authority by stooping to our level and meeting our needs. That's the authority we demonstrate to the people we lead. So we must ask ourselves: "What kind of leader am I? Do I lead as the Gentiles lead—or do I lead like Jesus? Do I intimidate or inspire? Am I a boss or a servant?"

"Not that we lord it over your faith, but we work with you for your joy, because it is by faith you stand firm."

—2 CORINTHIANS 1:24

FOR FURTHER REFLECTION:

1. Why do you want to be a leader?

2. How are preeminence, proximity, and power on display in the way you lead?

3. In what ways might service establish your authority as a leader and mentor? Be specific.

4. What can you do this week to help you avoid the temptation to lead as "the rulers of the Gentiles" did during Jesus's time? Make a list of at least five ideas.

6

Light Switch
or Panic Button?

Genesis 12

BENJAMIN HARRISON WAS PRESIDENT OF THE UNITED States from 1889 to 1893. He and his wife Caroline were the first couple to occupy the White House after it was wired for electricity. President Harrison had faced death many times as a Civil War general, but he and his wife were deathly afraid of a household appliance that you and I take for granted: a light switch.

President and Mrs. Harrison feared this strange new power source called electricity. What if they touched the light switch— and lightning jumped out of the wall to electrocute them?

So they relied on the White House servants to turn the lights on and off. If there were no servants on hand when the Harrisons retired for the night, they slept with the lights on.

A leader must have courage—but irrational fear can drive a leader to do irrational things. What is God's antidote to fear? Faith. God calls us to turn on the light switch of faith. All too often, instead of turning on the light switch, we press the panic button. That's what an Old Testament leader named Abraham did in Genesis 12.

Abraham's name at this stage of his life was Abram. (God changed his named to Abraham, "father of many nations," when Abram was ninety-nine years old; see Genesis 17:5.) When a severe famine came upon the land of Canaan, Abram went to Egypt, where there was plenty of food. Abram was a man with flocks and herds, and when the rains failed, his livelihood suffered.

God had called Abram to live in Canaan. When famine came upon the land, Abram took counsel, not from God, but from his fears. He pushed the panic button and fled to Egypt. Fear drove him out of the land God had promised to him.

Canaan symbolizes a life of fellowship with Jesus Christ. A famine in the land symbolizes any circumstance that threatens our fellowship with Him. Have you ever experienced a famine in your relationship with Christ? When we feel cut off from Him, we become fearful and we're tempted to flee instead of remaining in the Promised Land and trusting God to provide for us. We would rather go to "Egypt" where life seems more pleasant. Our escape to "Egypt" can take many forms.

Some escape through drugs, alcohol, overeating, overspending, gambling, or other addictions. Some immerse themselves in a whirling social life. Some choose a sexual affair or pornography. Some seek money, status, or fame.

It's not wrong to seek a momentary escape through times of rest and recreation. God understands that we need to recharge our physical and spiritual batteries. As Jesus said, "Come with me by yourselves to a quiet place and get some rest" (Mark 6:31). When we take time to rest with the Lord, we are retreating *more deeply* into Jesus—*not* running away from Him and escaping into "Egypt."

Abram's flight to Egypt was a matter of fear versus faith. When we're afraid, God calls us to turn our fear over to Him. That's faith. When we rely on Him in total trust, there's no room for fear. Faith cancels fear. But when we are ruled by fear, our fear cancels our faith. Consider:

> As he was about to enter Egypt, he said to his wife Sarai, "I know what a beautiful woman you are. When the Egyptians see you, they will say, 'This is his wife.' Then they will kill me but will let you live. Say you are my sister, so that I will be treated well for your sake and my life will be spared because of you." (Genesis 12:11–13)

Because of Sarai's beauty, the Egyptians took notice and Pharaoh invited her to his palace. Abram went with Sarai, and the Egyptians treated him well because of Sarai. He grew rich in Egypt, acquiring herds, flocks, and servants. But prosperity is not always a sign of God's favor:

> But the Lord inflicted serious diseases on Pharaoh and his household because of Abram's wife Sarai. So Pharaoh summoned Abram. "What have you done to me?" he said. "Why didn't you tell me she was your wife? Why did you say, 'She is my sister,' so that I took her to be my wife? Now then, here is your wife. Take her and go!" Then Pharaoh gave orders about Abram to his men, and they sent him on his way, with his wife and everything he had. (Genesis 12:17–20)

Abram had turned away from faith. He had gone to Egypt to escape the pressure of famine in Canaan. In Egypt, there was food, comfort, and security. Abram acquired wealth—but it came at the price of his integrity. His wealth was built on a lie.

We are all prone to rationalize away our integrity for the sake of an easier or better life. Abram probably told himself, "Okay, I lied—but look at all the benefits of that lie! I'd much rather live in this mansion in Egypt than my old tent in Canaan."

But Abram had compromised his faith and sacrificed his integrity. The lie he told the Egyptians was not altogether false. Sarai was Abram's half-sister. She was the daughter of a woman who married Abram's father after Abram was born. So even though Abram and Sarai were genetically related, Abram's claim was a half-truth. But a half-truth is a total lie.

We pretend that if there's a little grain of truth mixed in with the lie, then the lie isn't so bad. But any attempt to mislead is a lie. Why do we lie to ourselves, to others, and to God? Our lies are usually prompted by fear.

Abram's fear took a steady toll on his integrity. First, because of fear of the famine in Canaan, he moved to Egypt. When he moved out of Canaan, he moved out of fellowship with God. When we leave the Promised Land and move away from the tent and the altar, the old self comes to the fore and assumes control of our lives.

Fear of the Egyptians drove Abram to invent a lie about his wife. By attempting to save himself from the Egyptians, Abram put his wife Sarai in real danger. Pharaoh, who was unaware that Sarai was Abram's wife, claimed Sarai for his harem. Abram's lie, which he invented for his own protection, put Sarai's virtue at risk. When we engage in cowardice and deceit, our loved ones often pay the price.

Learn from Abram. When you're afraid, don't hit the panic button. Instead, flip the light switch of faith. Don't flee from the Promised Land. Don't run to Egypt. Stay where God has planted you, remain in His presence, seek His face, pray for strength and courage to stand firm in your faith and obedience to God. Guard your faith and integrity. The people you lead are counting on you.

"Be strong and courageous. Do not be afraid or terrified because of them, for the LORD your God goes with you; he will never leave you nor forsake you." —DEUTERONOMY 31:6

FOR FURTHER REFLECTION:

1. What is your "Canaan"—the Promised Land where God has planted you as a leader? And what is your "Egypt"—the place that tempts you in times of stress or fear?

2. Be honest: When are you tempted to use half-truths in your role as a leader or mentor? And what will you do about that?

3. If Abraham himself were teaching on Genesis 12:11–20, what do you think his top three points would be?

4. How will Abraham's experience from Genesis 12:11–20 influence what you do as a leader this week? Write down five ideas.

7

The Leader in Conflict

Genesis 13

WHEN I WAS TRAINING FOR THE MINISTRY, I TRAVELED FOR
several months as an assistant to Dr. Harry A. Ironside, pastor
of the Moody Church in Chicago. I once heard Dr. Ironside
relate an experience from his early life. His mother took him to a
church meeting. During the meeting, conflict erupted between
two Christian men. The situation became so heated that the
men nearly came to blows. One man stood and shouted, "I don't
care what you do—I insist on my rights!"

An older man, who was partially deaf, leaned forward in his
chair, cupped his ear, and said, "What did you say, brother? You
demand your rights, do you? Brother, if you had your rights,
you'd be in hell. The Lord Jesus didn't come to get His rights—
He came to get His wrongs, and He got them."

The angry fellow blushed and tugged at his collar. "Brother,"
he said, "you're right. I've been foolish and selfish. I apologize.
Settle the matter as you think best."

Soon, there was perfect agreement where there had once
been bitter conflict. Why? Because a man who had initially
reacted in the flesh was reminded of what it means to have the

mind of Christ. That reminder changed his heart—and resolved the conflict.

Most people regard conflict as a bad thing, a situation to be avoided at all costs. But conflict isn't always sinful or destructive. Conflict often occurs when there are creative, constructive tensions in a family, an organization, a corporation, or a church. Effective leaders are those who resolve conflict according to God's principles.

In Genesis 13, we find a lesson in how a godly leader handles conflict. It's the story of a conflict between Abram (who will later be known as Abraham, "father of many nations") and his nephew Lot. After the temporary lapse of faith that took Abram from Canaan into Egypt, we find him back in the Promised Land. He's living in his tent and worshiping at his altar. He's enjoying the fullness of God's provision for his life.

But life in the Promised Land is an experience of continual conflict. This is true even for us as Christian leaders, living in in the "Promised Land" of the Christian life. If we stop moving forward with God, we slip backwards. We must press on from one victory to the next.

Life in the Promised Land is also an experience of choices and decisions. The decisions that confront us often bring us into conflict with others. In Genesis 13, Abram faced a decision that brought him into conflict with his nephew Lot:

> Now Lot, who was moving about with Abram, also had flocks and herds and tents. But the land could not support them while they stayed together, for their possessions were so great that they were not able to stay together. And quarreling arose between Abram's herders and Lot's. The Canaanites and Perizzites were also living in the land at that time. (Genesis 13:5–7)

The story of Abram's nephew Lot is summed up in one phrase: "Now Lot, who was moving about with Abram . . ." Wherever Abram went, Lot went along. When Abram stopped, Lot stopped. Abram had invited Lot to go with him to Canaan because he wanted to help his nephew. But Lot, because of a tendency to make poor choices, was frequently a hindrance to Abram.

Lot symbolizes a common sort of Christian who depends on others for faith and the motivation to act. These Christians don't seem to have their own walk with God. They lean on other Christians or on TV and radio preachers for their faith. They lack an intimate connection with God.

Both Abram and Lot had flocks and herds, plus hired hands who helped manage the livestock. Lot's hired hands kept getting into quarrels with Abram's hired hands. To make matters worse, Genesis tells us, "The Canaanites and Perizzites were also living in the land at that time." These were godless tribes who would have taken advantage of any conflict between Abram and Lot as an opportunity to attack. Abram understood the danger, so he proposed a solution:

> So Abram said to Lot, "Let's not have any quarreling between you and me, or between your herders and mine, for we are close relatives. Is not the whole land before you? Let's part company. If you go to the left, I'll go to the right; if you go to the right, I'll go to the left." (Genesis 13:8–9)

Abram acted preemptively, making sure that he resolved the conflict with his nephew before his enemies could strike. As believers, we must act preemptively, resolving conflicts before feelings of bitterness attack and destroy us from within.

Notice that Abram acted as a matter of family unity: "Let's not have any quarreling between you and me . . . for we are close relatives." They were kinsmen, bound together in the same stream of life. Kinsmen cannot injure kinsmen without harming the entire family.

The same is true in the body of Christ, the church. Fellow Christians are brothers and sisters, members of one family of faith. Unresolved conflict among Christians injures the entire body. Abram, in his godly wisdom, said, in effect, "Let's settle this matter now before it divides the family."

Then Abram did a magnificent, Christlike thing: He willingly surrendered his own rights. As Lot's uncle, as the leader, Abram was entitled to the greater portion, yet he gave Lot the first choice. Abram's selfless offer shows that the altar of worship was at work in his heart. Genesis tells us:

> Abram lived in the land of Canaan, while Lot lived among the cities of the plain and pitched his tents near Sodom. Now the people of Sodom were wicked and were sinning greatly against the LORD. . .
>
> So Abram went to live near the great trees of Mamre at Hebron, where he pitched his tents. There he built an altar to the LORD. (Genesis 13:12–13, 18)

Lot selfishly chose the better, richer land—but in time, the choice to live near Sodom would cause him heartache, destruction, and loss. Abram selflessly made the godly choice, and true to his character as a leader of faith, he built an altar to the Lord. The choice to resolve conflict by sacrificing our own selfish interests may not bring us the greenest pastures or the greatest wealth, but it will always bring us the richest rewards.

"Live in harmony with one another. Do not be proud, but be willing to associate with people of low position. Do not be conceited."
—ROMANS 12:16

FOR FURTHER REFLECTION:

1. Do you identify more with Abram or with Lot? Explain.

2. What situations are most likely to push you toward conflict with someone at your work, in your church, or in your family? Why?

3. What are your "rights" as a Christian leader and mentor? Defend your answer in light of Abraham's example.

4. What steps can you take this week—in your marriage, your family, your company, or your church—to follow Abraham's selfless example regarding conflict?

8

The Leader in Adversity

Genesis 37–50

SOMERSET MAUGHAM'S SHORT STORY "THE VERGER" IS A parable about the benefits of affliction. It's the story of Albert Edward Foreman, the verger (caretaker or janitor) at St. Peter's Church at Neville Square in London. Albert has been the verger for sixteen years, ever since he was twelve years old, and he expects to remain in that job until he dies.

One day, a new vicar takes over and calls Albert into his office. "I have discovered to my astonishment," the vicar says, "that you can neither read nor write."

"The last vicar knew that, sir," Albert replies. "He said it didn't make no difference."

The vicar offers to give Albert a few months to learn to read, but Albert says it would do no good. If he couldn't learn to read as a child, he'll never learn now.

"At a church like St. Peter's Neville Square," the vicar says, "we cannot have a verger who can neither read nor write. I'm afraid you must go."

"Yes sir, I quite understand. I shall hand in my resignation as soon as you've found somebody to take my place."

So Albert leaves the church and walks down the street—and an idea occurs to him. Days later, he opens a little newsstand, and it does well. Then he opens a second, and a third. Ten years later, he owns ten newsstands all around London.

One day, Albert is talking to his banker, who urges him to invest his savings of more than thirty thousand pounds in some stocks and bonds. The banker offers to draw up a list of recommended securities for Albert to consider—but Albert replies that the paperwork would do him no good since he can neither read nor write.

"That's the most extraordinary thing I ever heard," the banker says. "Do you mean to say that you've built up this business and amassed a fortune of thirty thousand pounds without being able to read or write? Just think—what would you be now if you had learned to read?"

"I can tell you what I'd be, sir," Albert replies. "I'd be verger of St. Peter's Neville Square."[1]

Albert's illiteracy cost him his job as the verger, yet it led him to a new career and success beyond his imagining. What seemed like adversity and a disadvantage—his inability to read and write—proved a blessing in disguise. We see this same principle in the life of Joseph in the Book of Genesis.

Joseph, the son of Jacob and Rachel, was born in the land of Canaan. Joseph's ten half-brothers resented him because Jacob favored him over them. Jacob fueled their sibling rivalry by giving Joseph a beautiful robe embroidered in many colors. (Jacob's example of unwise fatherhood is a lesson for all of us who are leaders in our homes. When we display favoritism among our children, we stir up rage and resentment that produces unimaginable sorrow.)

In Genesis 37, seventeen-year-old Joseph told his brothers about two dreams he had—dreams that depicted Joseph's father,

mother, and brothers bowing down to him. Those dreams infu-
riated Joseph's brothers, and they plotted to murder him. They
ambushed him, threw him in a cistern, and intended to leave
him to die. But one of his brothers, Reuben, talked the others
into selling Joseph to some slave traders who passed by on their
way to Egypt. Then the brothers broke their father's heart, telling Jacob that Joseph was killed by a wild animal.

The slave traders sold Joseph to an Egyptian official named
Potiphar. Because of Joseph's godly character, Potiphar elevated
Joseph to a leadership position over his staff of servants. But
Potiphar's wife repeatedly tried to seduce Joseph when her husband was away. Joseph was a young man of rock-solid integrity,
and said, "How then could I do such a wicked thing and sin
against God?" (Genesis 39:9). Enraged by his repeated refusals,
Potiphar's wife accused him of attempted rape. So Potiphar had
to imprison his most godly and trustworthy servant for a crime
he didn't commit.

In prison, Joseph did a favor for a fellow inmate, Pharaoh's
former chief cupbearer. Joseph interpreted the man's dream and
predicted that the man would be reinstated in Pharaoh's court.
The cupbearer promised to put in a good word for Joseph with
Pharaoh when he was reinstated, but instead, he forgot his
promise. Joseph languished in prison for two more years.

Joseph was a godly, upright young man who suffered one
injustice after another. Not only was he innocent, but he was
punished for his righteous choices. He was sold into slavery and
thrown into prison not because he sinned, but because he was
a godly, morally upright young man. As someone once said,
"No good deed goes unpunished," and this statement was never
more true than in the life of Joseph.

One night, Pharaoh awoke in terror and told his wise men
about two dreams he'd had. None of them could interpret

the dreams. Then the cupbearer remembered Joseph and told Pharaoh about his former cellmate—Joseph, the interpreter of dreams. Pharaoh brought Joseph out of the prison, and Joseph interpreted the dreams: Egypt would have seven good years followed by seven years of drought and famine. Joseph's advice: Store some of the grain harvest from the good years so the Egyptian people would have food in the lean years.

Amazed at Joseph's wisdom, Pharaoh elevated Joseph, making him prime minister, the second most powerful leader in Egypt. Pharaoh placed a signet ring on Joseph's finger, a chain of gold around his neck, and royal robes on his shoulders.

When Joseph received his promotion from the dungeon to the palace, he was thirty years old. He had begun his journey of adversity at age seventeen. He'd spent *thirteen years*—his entire adult life—as either a slave or a prisoner. Yet it was his trial of adversity that directly led to his elevation to leadership. Without those thirteen years of adversity, he would never have been elevated to the second-in-command over all of Egypt.

In time, when famine overshadowed Egypt and Joseph's home country of Canaan, Joseph's brothers came to Egypt for help. The brothers met Joseph face to face, but didn't recognize him. When he revealed himself to them, and they realized the brother they had sold as a slave now held the power of life and death over them, they quaked in their sandals.

But Joseph forgave them and spoke these beautiful words to them: "You intended to harm me, but God intended it for good to accomplish what is now being done, the saving of many lives" (Genesis 50:20). The adversity his brothers had inflicted on him had been used by God to exalt Joseph as a wise and benevolent leader in the land of the Pharaohs.

So it is with you and me. The very obstacles we face in life, the very people who make us miserable and do us harm, are used by God to accomplish His good purpose in our lives. Joseph symbolizes the hope of all believers. What do we look forward to after death? Deliverance from the darkness and pain of this earthly existence, and from the prison in which we have lived our years—deliverance and exaltation to the very throne and presence of God himself.

Joseph is an Old Testament symbol of Jesus the Messiah: He was beloved of his father but rejected by his brothers, and he was sold into slavery for twenty pieces of silver. He seemingly died and was "brought to life" again as a triumphant king instead of a suffering servant. Like our Lord, Joseph forgave his brothers for their treatment of him and he was used to save them from death and preserve the family line.

God led Joseph through deep waters and dark places, through slavery, betrayal, false accusation, and unjust imprisonment—and Joseph's trust in God never wavered. God eventually exalted Joseph and fulfilled His word in everything He had promised.

The story of Joseph ends with the words, "So Joseph died at the age of a hundred and ten. And after they embalmed him, he was placed in a coffin in Egypt" (Genesis 50:26). Even in death, Joseph needed one last act of deliverance from God. His bones lay in a coffin in Egypt, and he needed to have his mortal remains delivered out of Egypt and taken up to the Promised Land. For that to happen, God would have to raise up another Hebrew leader in Egypt—but that's *another* story.

"The righteous person may have many troubles, but the LORD delivers him from them all." —PSALM 34:19

"And the God of all grace, who called you to his eternal glory in Christ, after you have suffered a little while, will himself restore you and make you strong, firm and steadfast."

—1 PETER 5:10

FOR FURTHER REFLECTION:

1. When have you felt like Joseph—punished for doing the right thing? How did you respond?

2. God allows bad things to happen to good people, even righteous people like Joseph. When that happens, what are your options?

3. When has God used adversity to create something good in your life? What happened?

4. How do you aspire to respond to adversity? What can you do tomorrow to help make that happen in the weeks to come?

9

The Reluctant Leader

Exodus 3–12

I ONCE VISITED THE HARRY S. TRUMAN LIBRARY AND Museum in Independence, Missouri. The former president was still living at the time, and it was said that he frequently went to the library and often greeted visitors in person. I had hoped to encounter Mr. Truman during my visit.

After the tour, I asked an attendant, "Has Mr. Truman been here today?"

"Yes," he replied. "Mr. Truman was here this morning."

I was sorry I had missed him. I would have asked him to tell me about the day he became President of the United States. It was a sad day in American history—April 12, 1945. Mr. Truman had been Vice President for fewer than a hundred days when the news flashed around the world that President Franklin D. Roosevelt had died of a sudden stroke.

With the death of FDR, Harry S. Truman became president. The day after taking the oath of office, President Truman spoke to reporters. "Boys," he said, "if you ever pray, pray for me now. I don't know if you fellows ever had a load of hay fall on you, but when they told me what happened yesterday, I felt like the moon, the stars, and all the planets had fallen on me."

Mr. Truman took office humbly and reluctantly, but with a strong sense of duty and purpose. Though he was reluctant to shoulder the burdens of the presidency, I think the title of Most Reluctant Leader of All Time goes to Moses, the deliverer of Israel.

The first two chapters of Exodus form a transition from the story of Joseph in Genesis to the story of Moses. We learn that, after the death of Joseph, the Israelites—the descendants of Joseph's father Jacob—became numerous. A new Egyptian king arose who did not know Joseph. Fearing the Israelites, this new Pharaoh ordered the slaughter of Hebrew male children.

When Moses was born, his mother hid him in a basket and set him afloat along the banks of the Nile. Pharaoh's daughter found the basket, rescued baby Moses, and raised him in the palace as her own. In Exodus 2, Moses killed an Egyptian who was beating a Hebrew slave. Fearing punishment, Moses escaped to the wilderness of Midian, where he lived as a shepherd.

There, God came to Moses and called him to lead His people out of bondage. Speaking to Moses from a burning bush, God challenged Moses and instructed him to return to Egypt. But Moses refused. "Pardon your servant, Lord," he said, "I have never been eloquent, neither in the past nor since you have spoken to your servant. I am slow of speech and tongue" (Exodus 4:10).

God didn't rebuke Moses for his reluctance to lead. Instead, God said, "Who gave human beings their mouth? Who makes them deaf or mute? . . . Is it not I, the LORD? Now go; I will help you speak and will teach you what to say." Moses expressed self-doubt and a humble sense of inadequacy—and God will never rebuke a humble spirit.

But even after God had assured Moses, "I will help you

speak," Moses was *still* reluctant. "Pardon your servant, Lord," he said. "Please send someone else."

At this point, the Lord became angry with Moses. Why? Because Moses was no longer doubting himself. He was doubting God. Moses said, in effect, "God, I can't do this—and I don't believe I can do it even in Your strength. Send someone else." When Moses doubted God's adequacy to be his strength, he crossed the line from humility to unbelief.

The Lord said, "What about your brother, Aaron the Levite? I know he can speak well. He is already on his way to meet you, and he will be glad to see you. You shall speak to him and put words in his mouth; I will help both of you speak and will teach you what to do. He will speak to the people for you."

God appears to hand the responsibility to Aaron—yet, throughout the rest of the account, it is Moses who ultimately exercises leadership, and Aaron's role is clearly secondary. God gave Moses the option of using Aaron as his spokesman— yet God knew all along that Moses would grow in his faith and confidence in the Lord. Even though "the LORD's anger burned against Moses" because of Moses's unbelief, God loved Moses and fully intended to use him to deliver the people from bondage.

Moses returned to Egypt and challenged Pharaoh. There is no more dramatic scene in the Old Testament than the test of wills between Pharaoh and Moses. It's a clash between the representative of Satan and the representative of God. Ultimately, Pharaoh forces God to unleash His power against Egypt. Again and again we read, "Pharaoh hardened his heart."

There were ten plagues in all: blood, frogs, lice, flies, disease on the animals, boils on people and animals, hail, locusts, darkness, and finally, death of the firstborn sons. Each of the first nine plagues is directed at one of the false gods of Egypt and designed to show the worthlessness of Egypt's pagan religious system. The tenth plague is aimed at Pharaoh himself, striking Pharaoh's son and all the firstborn sons of Egypt. It is God's attempt to melt Pharaoh's heart of stone.

After Pharaoh loses his son in the tenth plague, his stubborn heart is finally overcome. Pharaoh relents—and he tells Moses to go and take his people with him. During this tenth plague, God's power and love are dramatically revealed—power to punish oppressors and love toward those who trust Him and obey.

During the tenth plague, the beautiful tradition of Passover was celebrated for the first time—a tradition the Jewish people still celebrate today. God commanded His people to sprinkle a lamb's blood on the doorposts of their houses and to share a special meal of lamb with unleavened bread—the Passover supper. This event is a beautiful Old Testament foreshadowing of a New Testament truth. By receiving the gift of eternal life through the shedding of the blood of Jesus on the "doorposts" of the cross, by partaking of the innocent Lamb and the unleavened bread of His broken body, we become a part of Him. His blood delivers us from death.

At the first Passover, the Lord passed through the land, darkening Egypt with death. But the Israelites, taking shelter beneath the shed blood of the lamb, were safe. Then and now, salvation is accomplished by simple faith, a trusting response to God's loving provision of a Savior who has removed our guilt from God's sight.

God chose Moses to stand before Pharaoh—that's why God made sure baby Moses would be found by the riverbank and raised in Pharaoh's palace. God chose Moses despite his reluctance, excuses, and unbelief. The last job title in the world Moses wanted was "leader." He was content to while away his days in the desert, tending sheep.

Are you a reluctant leader? Are you making excuses to God? If you doubt yourself, if you lack confidence, that's fine, God gives grace to the humble (James 4:6). But don't doubt God and His power. Say "yes" to God's call. When He chooses you, step up and lead.

"I am the LORD, the God of all mankind. Is anything too hard for me?" —JEREMIAH 32:27

"I can do all this through him who gives me strength." —PHILIPPIANS 4:13

FOR FURTHER REFLECTION:

1. What makes you feel reluctant to lead? Why?

2. God orchestrated events in Moses's life that prepared him to lead. How have you seen God do the same in your life? Be specific.

3. True or false: A person can say no when God's calls him or her to lead? Defend your answer.

4. What does it take to become a leader or mentor like Moses—someone who hears God's direction and trusts God for the results? Brainstorm a list.

10

The Confident Leader

Exodus 14

DR. MARTIN LUTHER KING, JR. OFTEN CITED MOSES AS A role model and inspirational figure during the troubled years of the civil rights movement. Dr. King delivered his final sermon at the Bishop Charles Mason Temple in Memphis, Tennessee, on April 3, 1968. In that speech, he talked about the example set by Moses.

"If I were standing at the beginning of time," he said, "with the possibility of a general and panoramic view of the whole human history up to now, and the Almighty said to me, 'Martin Luther King, which age would you like to live in?'—I would take my mental flight by Egypt through, or rather across the Red Sea, through the wilderness on toward the Promised Land." He went on to describe other moments in history when oppressed people gained their freedom.

At the end of his talk, he returned to thoughts of Moses, saying, "We've got some difficult days ahead. But it doesn't matter with me now. Because I've been to the mountaintop. And I don't mind. Like anybody, I would like to live a long life. Longevity has its place. But I'm not concerned about that now.

I just want to do God's will. And He's allowed me to go up to the mountain. And I've looked over. And I've seen the Promised Land. I may not get there with you. But I want you to know tonight, that we, as a people will get to the Promised Land. And I'm happy, tonight. I'm not worried about anything. I'm not fearing any man. Mine eyes have seen the glory of the coming of the Lord."

The next day, April 4, 1968, Dr. King was slain by an assassin's bullet.

The leadership journey of Moses has inspired many leaders through the years. It instructs you and me in our leadership lives today. We have looked at the story of Moses up to the Passover—but the Passover is just part of the story. The Passover has no value apart from the Red Sea experience. To understand the leadership model of Moses, we cannot stop with the Passover. We must press on to the Red Sea.

When Pharaoh released the people of Israel, they went out into the wilderness and walked to the shore of the Red Sea. They were still on the Egyptian side of the sea when they looked behind them and saw Pharaoh and his army coming after them. The people cried out to Moses, "What have you done to us by bringing us out of Egypt? . . . It would have been better for us to serve the Egyptians than to die in the desert!" (Exodus 14:11–12).

Moses replied, "Do not be afraid. Stand firm and you will see the deliverance the LORD will bring you today. The Egyptians you see today you will never see again. The LORD will fight for you; you need only to be still" (Exodus 14:13–14).

Though Moses's faith in God was strong, he had misunderstood God's instructions when he told the people, "You need only to be still." God told Moses that he didn't want the people to "be still." God wanted the people to *move*. He told Moses,

"Why are you crying out to me? *Tell the Israelites to move on.*
Raise your staff and stretch out your hand over the sea to divide
the water so that the Israelites can go through the sea on dry
ground" (Exodus 14:15–16, emphasis added).

Then God's angel and a pillar of cloud that had gone before
the people moved behind them to serve as a barrier between the
Israelites and the pursuing Egyptians. The angel and the pillar
of cloud caused darkness to fall upon the Egyptians, while it
remained light on the Israelite side. Then Moses stretched his
hand out over the sea, and God sent a strong wind to divide
the waters. Then the Israelites walked across the seabed on dry
ground, with the waters piled high on either side of them.

The Red Sea experience was an event in human history, and
it is also a powerful symbol for your life and mine. It typifies
our break with the world, once we have placed our trust in Jesus
Christ. Egypt is behind us; the journey to the Promised Land
is before us. The Israelites were safely out of Egypt and out of
bondage. They had passed through the waters of death.

The same waters of death roll between us and the world once
we claim Jesus Christ as our Lord. When we pass through our
own Red Sea through the sacrament of baptism, we symbolically
die to the old life and our former bondage. As Paul tells us, "If
anyone is in Christ, the new creation has come; the old has
gone, the new is here!" (2 Corinthians 5:17).

The people of Israel became a nation when they passed
through the Red Sea together. That is the meaning of Paul's
statement in 1 Corinthians 10:2, "They were all baptized into
Moses in the cloud and in the sea." By this miraculous baptism,
they were transformed into a mighty nation.

The Passover and the crossing of the Red Sea are linked
together. Both events involve faith, but the Red Sea crossing
takes faith one step further. The Israelites were passive recipients

of their Passover deliverance. They painted the doorposts with blood, they ate their meal, and they waited for God to act. But the crossing of the Red Sea was active, it required the people to take an obedient step of faith and *move*.

True faith still requires both action and obedience. We cannot remain Passover-passive. We must move ahead as God commands, boldly trusting Him to part the waters and lead the way. As we cut our ties to the bondage of this world and step out in faith in God, our faith takes on substance and power. God cannot bring us to maturity until we have passed through the Red Sea.

"When you pass through the waters, I will be with you; and when you pass through the rivers, they will not sweep over you. When you walk through the fire, you will not be burned; the flames will not set you ablaze." —ISAIAH 43:2

FOR FURTHER REFLECTION:

1. Describe in your own words the leadership journey of Moses. What do you want to remember?

2. As a Christian leader, how do you know when to be still before God, and when to move forward with God? Explain it as a set of principles that could be used as a guide.

3. It took all night for God to divide the waters. What goes on inside you when you're waiting for God to work on your behalf?

4. Complete this sentence: *For me to become a leader who is more like Moses, tomorrow I must . . .*

11

Preparing for Leadership

Exodus 17; Numbers 13–14; Joshua 1

ABRAHAM LINCOLN WAS AN UNKNOWN ILLINOIS PRAIRIE lawyer when someone asked him if he had political ambitions. "I will prepare myself and be ready," the future president replied. "Perhaps my chance will come."

The story of Joshua is the account of another leader who prepared himself. When his chance came, Joshua, the son of Nun, the disciple of Moses, was ready. Joshua is a great biblical role model for leaders. These times call for righteous, courageous leaders who can stand up to the pressures and hostility of this world.

We first meet Joshua in Exodus 17. The Israelites were wandering through the wilderness on their long journey from Egypt to the Promised Land. At a place called Rephidim, the Amalekites attacked. Moses placed Joshua in charge of the army of Israel, telling him, "Choose some of our men and go out to fight the Amalekites. Tomorrow I will stand on top of the hill with the staff of God in my hands."

So Joshua led the army against the Amalekites while Moses, aided by Aaron and Hur, stood atop a hill, with the rod of the

Lord raised in his hand. The battle raged for hours. Whenever Moses's arms grew tired and he could no longer hold the rod aloft, the Amalekites began to prevail. Aaron and Hur helped Moses by adding their strength, raising Moses's arms higher. In the end, Joshua and his army defeated the Amalekites.

Moses mentored Joshua and trained him to be his successor as the leader of Israel. Joshua went with Moses up Mount Sinai when Moses received the tablets of the Ten Commandments. Joshua was also one of the twelve spies Moses sent to survey the land of Canaan in Numbers 13. When only Joshua and his comrade Caleb gave a positive report (the other ten warned against entering Canaan), God rewarded Joshua and Caleb for their faith—and punished the rest of that unfaithful generation. God said, "In this wilderness your bodies will fall—every one of you twenty years old or more who was counted in the census and who has grumbled against me. Not one of you will enter the land . . . except Caleb . . . and Joshua" (Numbers 14:29–30).

There is a powerful lesson here for our own Christian lives. Often, we find that it's not until we come to the end of ourselves and must make a new beginning in our lives that we allow the Spirit to take over and lead us into our own Land of Promise. That's why so many Christians never seem to find victory until they have a crisis experience followed by a new beginning. God says, "Trust Me," but we resist and resist. God has to knock all the props out from under us. When we have nothing left to cling to but Him, we cry out, "God, You're my only hope!" Then He can say, "Now I can bless you as I have always longed to bless you."

In Joshua 1:1–9, God appointed Joshua as the successor to Moses. So Moses summoned Joshua and gave him this solemn charge: "Be strong and courageous, for you must go with this people into the land that the LORD swore to their ancestors to give them, and you must divide it among them as their inheritance. The LORD himself goes before you and will be with you; he will never leave you nor forsake you. Do not be afraid; do not be discouraged" (Deuteronomy 31:7–8).

From the summit of Mount Nebo, Moses looked out on the horizon of Canaan, the Promised Land. Then Moses died and was buried in the land of Moab, and Joshua took command. After the death of Moses, when Joshua faced the lonely challenge of leading the nation of Israel, God spoke to Joshua and told him the secret of confidence and faith in the Lord:

> "Keep this Book of the Law always on your lips; meditate on it day and night, so that you may be careful to do everything written in it. Then you will be prosperous and successful. Have I not commanded you? Be strong and courageous. Do not be afraid; do not be discouraged, for the LORD your God will be with you wherever you go." (Joshua 1:8–9)

By meditating in the Scriptures, we gain confidence and courage to meet the challenges of leadership. The Scriptures remind us that God is with us wherever we go. Meditate in the Word, follow God with confidence, make bold decisions, lead courageously, don't be afraid or discouraged. That is God's spiritual pep talk to Joshua as he shoulders this new responsibility.

The name "Joshua" is significant. It's the Hebrew form of a name that you know quite well in its Greek form: "Jesus." That's right—Joshua in the Old Testament had the same name as Jesus in the New Testament. The symbolism is too obvious to miss.

The five books of Moses were written to bring the people to the edge of the Land of Promise, but Moses could not take the people into the land. Moses represented the Law. As Paul said in Romans 8:3, "What the law was powerless to do because it was weakened by the flesh, God did by sending his own Son." Only Joshua could lead his people into the physical Land of Promise, the land of Canaan. And it is the new Joshua—Jesus the Messiah—who leads us into the eternal Land of Promise, our heavenly home.

"Remember your leaders, who spoke the word of God to you. Consider the outcome of their way of life and imitate their faith."
—HEBREWS 13:7

FOR FURTHER REFLECTION:

1. What do you think was the most important factor in Joshua's preparation for leadership? Why?

2. What leadership principles do you see at play in the account of the Israelites' battle against the Amalekites? Make a list.

3. A leader like Joshua can find strength, confidence, and courage in God—but how exactly does that work? Explain it.

4. What will you take from Joshua's example to help you lead or mentor others this week?

12

Joshua's Leadership Legacy

Joshua 6–8, 13, 24

DURING A VISIT TO ISRAEL, I DROVE TO THE SHOMRON Valley and stood in the shadow of the twin peaks of Mount Ebal and Mount Gerizim. As Joshua 8 records, that is the place where Joshua read the Book of the Law to all the people and renewed the covenant between God and the nation of Israel. Half of the people of Israel stood in front of Mount Ebal and half stood in front of Mount Gerizim. Joshua read a passage from Leviticus that promises blessings for those who keep God's Law—and penalties for those who violate the Law.

Those two mountains visually represented both the blessings and the penalties. Mount Ebal was the taller of the two mountains, and its bleak, rocky slopes were strewn with gray rubble. That desolate mountain represented the penalties that awaited those who would rebel against God's Law. Mount Gerizim, by contrast, had green, forested slopes. Beautiful Mount Gerizim represented God's blessings for those who remained faithful to His Law.

When Joshua took command of the nation of Israel, he became the leader of a people who had spent four centuries as slaves in Egypt. The people had never been trained in the art of warfare. They confronted a land populated with violent, warlike pagan tribes. Yet Joshua was able to organize his army into a mighty fighting force. When the Israelites swept into the land of Canaan, they quickly conquered the walled fortresses of the Canaanites, and won the land.

The first enemy the Israelites faced once they entered the Promised Land was Jericho—that walled super-fortress of a city. Their own weapons seemed feeble and useless compared with those unassailable walls. The people wondered, "How can we prevail over such a city?"

Have you ever faced an insurmountable obstacle? A task that's beyond your strength? An illness that won't go away? That is your Jericho. The siege of Jericho symbolizes the world in its assault on the Christian—and it symbolizes our Lord's victory over the world.

Joshua sent spies into Jericho. Rahab, a Canaanite prostitute, sheltered the spies inside the city, and they discovered that all of Canaan was in fear of Israel's God. At God's instruction, the Israelites marched around the city walls once a day for seven days, led by the priests and the Ark of the Covenant. On the seventh day, the people marched seven times around the walls—then the priests blew horns and the people shouted. The walls of the city fell, and the Israelites stormed into the city. Of the inhabitants, the Israelites spared only Rahab, as God commanded.

The victory at Jericho was followed by the defeat at Ai. The irony of these two incidents is that Jericho was a fortress while Ai was an insignificant little village, a wide spot in the road. Ai should have been an easy victory for Joshua and his army—yet the villagers of Ai handily defeated Joshua's army. Why? Because there was sin in the Israelite camp.

One of the Israelites, a man named Achan, had taken some

of the spoils of the victory at Jericho, in violation of God's command. Here we see that one believer's sin can bring defeat on an entire community. Until the Israelites dealt with the sin of Achan, they could not have victory over Ai.

The story of Ai symbolizes the danger of seemingly "minor" sins. We think sins like anger, bitterness, lust, and evil thoughts won't hurt anyone. Who will ever know? But those "hidden" sins have a way of becoming a Christian's Achilles' heel—the very sin that brings a believer down in sorrow and disgrace. Sins of the flesh not only produce tragic defeat in our own lives, but can bring hurt to the people around us.

The theme of the Book of Joshua is set forth in Joshua 13:1: "When Joshua had grown old, the LORD said to him, 'You are now very old, and there are still very large areas of land to be taken over.'" The peril Israel faced is common to us all: the temptation to stop short of complete victory. We say, "I know I haven't conquered all the sins in my life, but I've come so far. Lord, let me rest here. No more battles. Let me keep these sins just a while longer." That's the enemy's subtle attack whenever we experience a spiritual victory.

Jesus said, "Blessed are those who hunger and thirst for righteousness, for they will be filled" (Matthew 5:6). Our lives should be marked by a hunger and a thirst for the righteousness of God. Until the war is won and God calls us to a place of rest in the Land of Promise, we are on a war footing. We must see the battle through to victory—or the battle will be lost. If we lose our individual battles with sin, we may, like Achan, bring harm to the people we love.

Near the end of his life, Joshua warned the people against moral and spiritual compromise, because they still had land to conquer and possess. He exhorted them to "choose for yourselves this day whom you will serve, whether the gods your ancestors served beyond the Euphrates or the gods of the Amorites, in whose land you are living. But as for me and my household, we will serve the LORD" (Joshua 24:15).

Joshua was relentless in his faith and obedience. He was on the march, serving the Lord until the day he died. That was his leadership legacy to you and me. What kind of leadership legacy are we bequeathing to the people around us?

"Blessed is the one who perseveres under trial because, having stood the test, that person will receive the crown of life that the Lord has promised to those who love him." —JAMES 1:12

FOR FURTHER REFLECTION:

1. What principles of success do you see in Joshua's experience? List at least three.

2. What is the great obstacle—the "Jericho"—that blocks your potential success in leadership? What clue do you find in the life of Joshua to help overcome that Jericho?

3. How do you suppose Joshua would advise you when dealing with defeat? What would you do with his advice?

4. What leadership legacy do you want to bequeath to the people around you? How will you add to that legacy this week?

13

The Humble Leader

Judges 7

HUDSON TAYLOR WAS A PIONEERING MISSIONARY TO CHINA and the founder of the China Inland Mission (now OMF International). He spent more than half a century in China, brought more than 800 missionaries to China and helped found more than a hundred schools and hundreds of churches in all eighteen provinces of China.

Taylor once spoke at an Australian church and was embarrassed by the glowing introduction the pastor gave him, referring to Taylor as "our illustrious guest." With characteristic humility, Taylor began, "Dear friends, I am the little servant of an illustrious Master."

God loves humble people. I'm always impressed, as I study the Scriptures, how many times God passes over the proud, the mighty, the powerful, and selects some obscure individual to accomplish His purposes. He always chooses the humble over the proud.

Gideon, in the book of Judges, was a humble, obscure leader—the kind of leader God uses. He lived in the times of the Judges, when Israel suffered oppression at the hands of the

Midianites. The enemy attacked the Israelites, ruined their crops, and stole their livestock, forcing the Israelites to hide in mountain clefts and caves.

God called upon Gideon and told him to deliver Israel from the Midianites. Gideon was so sure he didn't amount to anything that he demanded proof that God had truly called *him* to deliver Israel. Gideon thought God had called him by mistake.

Gideon set a wool fleece upon the floor one night and told God, in effect, "If there's dew on top of this fleece when I wake up in the morning, I'll know you called me." The next morning, Gideon got up and wrung the dew out of the fleece—and there was a whole bowl full of water. Even so, Gideon was not sure. He asked God to confirm it once more the next night—only this time, he asked God to make the dew appear underneath the fleece and let the top side be dry. Again, God confirmed that He had chosen this humble man.

So Gideon assembled an army to attack the Midianites. He started with 32,000 men. Then, at God's direction, he whittled that force down to the men who showed no sign of fear— 10,000 men. Then, at God's direction, he reduced that force to the men who drank water from a stream in such a way that they were always alert—a mere 300 men. With that seemingly insignificant force of soldiers, led by a self-effacing leader named Gideon, the tiny Israelite army defeated the Midianite army—a force of 135,000 well-armed soldiers.

Gideon and his men approached the Midianite camp at night. He overheard one of the Midianite soldiers tell a friend about his dream in which a loaf of barley bread tumbled into the Midianite camp, destroying the camp (Judges 7:13). Gideon interpreted this man's dream to mean that God had given the Midianites over to the small Israelite force. Gideon gave each of his men a shofar (a trumpet) and a clay jar. They hid candles inside the clay jars.

Then Gideon divided his force into three groups. Gideon and his men approached the Midianite camp. On his order, they blew their trumpets, shouted a battle cry, broke the clay jars, and exposed the lighted candles. To the Midianites, it seemed they were surrounded by thousands of soldiers. They panicked and began to kill each other—and the survivors fled in terror (Judges 7:17–22).

The apostle Paul might have been thinking of Gideon's rout of the Midianites when he wrote, "But we have this treasure in jars of clay to show that this all-surpassing power is from God and not from us" (2 Corinthians 4:7). An earthen jar is a beautiful image of our humanity. We were made to contain God. Our Creator designed us so that God's power might shine in us like candles in an earthen jar.

Gideon's army, in obedience to God's command, took earthen jars—common pots of clay—and put lighted candles in them. God has placed His all-surpassing power within us, power to terrorize our enemies. Though they outnumber us, God will set them to flight—and the victory will be ours.

God used a humble, self-effacing leader named Gideon to defeat a vastly superior force. He made Gideon pare his army down to only 300 men to show that victory came from the power of God, not superior numbers or force. God would not use Gideon's army until it was small enough to be of no effect.

In the same way, Jesus was best able to use the apostle Peter only after Peter had failed Him in a major way. When Peter walked with Jesus, he was proud, boastful, and impetuous. He would compare himself to the other disciples and seemingly say, "Lord, look at these other fellows; you can't count on them. But you can always count on me. I'll never let you down!"

Later, this same boastful Peter denied Jesus three times—then went out into the streets of Jerusalem, weeping bitterly over his failure. Humiliated, defeated, no longer sure of himself, Peter felt unworthy to call himself a follower of Jesus. It was only then that Jesus finally entrusted him with a sacred duty: "Peter, feed my lambs" (John 21:15).

God rarely uses anyone in a great way until He has taken that person through failure. Why? God wants His servants to be emptied of pride and ego, and able to empathize with the least and the last and the lost, the ones He seeks to save.

Have you been humbled? Have you been humiliated by failure? Do you feel foolish and weak? Then you're ready to be used by God. The humble, the obscure, the self-effacing person—that's the leader God uses.

"But he gives us more grace. That is why Scripture says: 'God opposes the proud but shows favor to the humble.'" —JAMES 4:6

FOR FURTHER REFLECTION:

1. Why does God choose to use humble people? Brainstorm a list of ideas.

2. What do you suppose went through Gideon's mind as God cut his army from 32,000 men to 10,000 men to a mere 300 men? How would you have responded to that?

3. "God opposes the proud but shows favor to the humble" (James 4:6). When have you seen that happen? Describe that experience.

4. What would you say are five hallmarks of a humble, yet effective, leader? How can you pursue those qualities this week?

14

Leading in the Flesh or by Faith?

---

1 Samuel 8–13

WHETHER YOU LEAD A NATION, A CORPORATION, A CHURCH, or a family, whether you are young or old, man or woman, in the secular world or in Christian ministry, it's vitally important that you answer this question in your own heart: Do you lead in the flesh—or by faith?

In 1 Samuel 8, the elders of Israel confronted the prophet Samuel with a demand that he anoint a king to lead the nation, such as other nations had. Israel had never had a king. Instead, Israel had enjoyed direct fellowship with God.

But the principle of the flesh was at work in the nation of Israel. The worldly mindset of the people cut Israel off from fellowship with God. They rejected His authority in favor of a human king—the same kind of authority all the worldly nations had. The flesh always desires to live in a manner accepted by the world,

You've probably seen this principle at work in your church. Some people want to run the church according to worldly business principles. Others want to run the church according to the principles of Scripture. Instead of relying on the leadership of the Holy Spirit, we often prefer to appoint a committee to devise a program. Then we ask God to bless our program and make it work. The problem is that it's a humanly designed program, based on the "wisdom" of the world, not God's program, based on faith.

Someone once said, "Be careful what you ask for—you may get it." The people of Israel demanded a human king and God gave them one. Samuel was displeased when the people asked for a king, because he knew it was not God's plan. But the Lord told Samuel, "Listen to all that the people are saying to you; it is not you they have rejected, but they have rejected me as their king. As they have done from the day I brought them up out of Egypt until this day, forsaking me and serving other gods, so they are doing to you" (1 Samuel 8:7–8).

If we want something badly enough, God will often give it to us—even if it's not His perfect will for our lives. Here's the catch: We must also be ready to accept the consequences.

God led Samuel to select a young man named Saul to lead Israel. Young Saul lived by the principle of the flesh, not the principle of faith. He did what *he* wanted to do, disregarding God's plan for his life. Before he was anointed king, Saul was in the donkey business. How did God reach Saul? He caused Saul's donkeys to stray, forcing Saul to set out in search of the donkeys. After a fruitless search, Saul reached the town where Samuel lived.

In chapter 9, Saul was about to give up and go back home when his servant said, "Look, in this town there is a man of God. . . Let's go there now. Perhaps he will tell us what way to take" (1 Samuel 9:6). The man of God was Samuel. Saul wanted nothing to do with the prophet Samuel. He just wanted to go home. But the servant prevailed on him to see Samuel—and to Saul's amazement, Samuel was expecting him.

God had told Samuel the day before to expect a visit from a young man named Saul. Samuel had a great dinner prepared for Saul and thirty invited guests. Saul was surprised to learn that he was the guest of honor. Samuel took Saul aside and said, "Has not the LORD anointed you ruler over his inheritance?" (1 Samuel 10:1).

Saul had been out looking for donkeys, but he ended up a king. He didn't even want the job! Saul was not interested in what God wanted him to do.

Samuel's next step was to announce to Israel that God had heard their plea and would give them a king. Samuel called the people together to cast lots for the choice of a king. Ultimately, the lot fell to Saul. So the people went looking for Saul and found him hiding among the baggage—an unlikely place to find a king.

Why did Saul hide? He didn't want to be inconvenienced by God's plan. Saul wanted to live his life his own way, and he was trying to get away from God's call.

Finally, he was crowned king—and he looked the very picture of a king. He stood head and shoulders above everyone else, handsome as could be. When the Ammonites made war against Israel, Saul assembled an army of 36,000 men. They marched north and destroyed the Ammonites—and Saul thought that serving God might be a good thing after all. Maybe he could use his position for his own glory.

Next, Saul went to war against the Philistines, the regional superpower of that era. When he saw the Philistine forces—30,000 chariots, 6,000 horsemen, and an army too vast to number—Saul wasn't so sure he wanted to be king after all. When he put out the call for volunteers, only 3,000 Hebrew soldiers showed up. Saul contrasted this pitiful force against the Philistine army, and he sent for the prophet Samuel. This is typical: The man of the flesh depends on his own resources until he gets into trouble—then he calls upon the Lord.

But Samuel was delayed in coming—and as Samuel delayed, Saul's men began to slip away and return home. Saul's army dwindled from 3,000 to 2,000, to 1,000. Saul became desperate. Finally, Saul took it upon himself to offer a burnt offering to the Lord. The moment he finished, Samuel came up and demanded to know, "What have you done?"

Saul replied that he was frightened by the size of the Philistine army, so he sought God's favor by offering a sacrifice to God.

"You have done a foolish thing," Samuel said. "You have not kept the command the LORD your God gave you; if you had, he would have established your kingdom over Israel for all time. But now your kingdom will not endure; the LORD has sought out a man after his own heart and appointed him ruler of his people, because you have not kept the LORD's command" (1 Samuel 13:13–14).

Saul's kingdom would be taken from him—yet God made Israel victorious over the Philistines through the faith of Saul's son Jonathan. After the battle, Saul built an altar. Like many Christians today, Saul thought that outward demonstrations of faith were adequate to win God's favor. We think God will be satisfied if we attend church, recite a creed, and sing Christian songs. That's the reasoning of the flesh.

The lesson of the life of Saul is that leaders who lead according to the flesh will lose their kingdom, their authority, their leadership role. But those who lead by faith will be commended by God.

"Those who live according to the flesh have their minds set on what the flesh desires; but those who live in accordance with the Spirit have their minds set on what the Spirit desires. The mind governed by the flesh is death, but the mind governed by the Spirit is life and peace." —ROMANS 8:5–6

FOR FURTHER REFLECTION:

1. In what ways do you identify with Saul as a leader? Explain.

2. What causes you, like Saul, to feel reluctant to lead? How do you handle those situations?

3. What is the most important decision you ever made as a leader? In what ways did God's Holy Spirit lead through that decision? Describe it.

4. Make a list to finish this sentence: "A leadership decision made in accordance with the Spirit shows these qualities . . ." What will you do with your list this week?

15

The Rebellious Leader

1 Samuel 15

I ONCE READ ABOUT A MAN WHO WAS STOPPED BY A POLICE officer for speeding. When the officer handed him the ticket, the man read it, tossed it back at the officer, threw his car into gear, and sped off. The officer jumped into his car and pursued the lawbreaker at high speeds. The man ran his car off the road, rolled it, and killed both himself and his six-year-old daughter who was riding in the car with him.

This man was an ordinary middle-class suburbanite who, I'm sure, did not consider himself a criminal. What made him suddenly rebel against the law in such an extreme and deadly way? I believe it was the innate rebelliousness within every human heart when confronted by authority. That same rebelliousness lurks in us all. This man took it to a fatal extreme.

People often say to me in counseling: "I know what I ought to do, but I don't want to do it." Why don't they do what they know is right? Humanity is rebellious at heart. In the story of King Saul, we see the exposed heart of a rebellious leader—and we see the tragic consequences when his rebellion is taken to a fatal extreme.

Our God is a God of second chances. Despite Saul's past failures, God was not through with him. After Saul built an altar in his own self-will, God sent Samuel to command Saul to destroy the Amalekites for making war against Israel. Saul was to completely destroy the enemy, including all the people and all their animal herds.

This was Saul's last chance to get it right, his last chance to lead by faith instead of the flesh. If Saul obeyed, he would demonstrate he was ready to allow the Spirit of God to lead through him.

Throughout Scripture, the Amalekites are a symbolic picture of human pride and sinful flesh that opposes the things of God. Five centuries earlier, Moses had prophesied to Israel, "The LORD will be at war against the Amalekites from generation to generation" (Exodus 17:16). God gave Saul one last opportunity to carry out His will by obliterating the Amalekites. What did Saul do?

Saul obeyed halfway. He carried out God's command—but he insisted on doing it his way, according to his own fleshly will. He slaughtered the Amalekites—but he spared King Agag of the Amalekites, and he spared the best of the sheep, cattle, lambs, and calves. He kept all the fat, healthy, valuable livestock for himself.

You might be horrified by God's command to destroy the Amalekites. But it's important to understand who the Amalekites were. Deuteronomy 12:31 tells us that the Amalekites and other Canaanite tribes committed unthinkable atrocities against their own children: ". . . In worshiping their gods, they do all kinds of detestable things the LORD hates. They even burn their sons and daughters in the fire as sacrifices to their gods.".

Archaeologists confirm that the Amalekites and neighboring tribes placed children alive in the arms of bronze idols and sent them tumbling into a furnace in the belly of the idol. Other children were suffocated in jars as sacrifices to their gods. The Lord commanded the destruction of the Amalekites and their demonic religion *not* out of cruelty, but out of mercy for the Amalekite children.

Saul's decision to obey God halfway, and to keep the livestock and spare the Amalekite king, was a decision of the flesh. Saul, who was a donkey herder in his early life, couldn't bring himself to slaughter perfectly good farm animals—even though God had condemned the animals to destruction.

You and I are a lot like Saul, are we not? We are willing to obey God—halfway. We are willing to put off the old nature, the nature of the flesh—up to a point. We will put certain sins to death. We may rid ourselves of jealousy, bitterness, envy, and selfishness, sins we don't care that much about. But what about anger? What about lust? I can't give up those sins!

The Spirit-controlled mind does not compromise with sin. The Spirit-controlled mind does not obey halfway. The mind that is controlled by God's Spirit obeys God to the Nth degree. But the mind of the flesh rationalizes and declares "good" what God has declared to be sin.

Saul told Samuel, "I have carried out the LORD's instructions."

But Samuel said, "What then is this bleating of sheep in my ears? What is this lowing of cattle that I hear?" (1 Samuel 15:13–14).

Then Saul admitted that he had "spared the best of the sheep and cattle to sacrifice to the LORD your God, but we totally destroyed the rest" (1 Samuel 15:15). That's the ultimate self-delusional rationalization: "Yes, I disobeyed God, but I'm going to dedicate these ill-gotten spoils to God! Even though I disobeyed, I really did a *good* thing!" But Samuel shuts down Saul's excuses and rationalizations:

Does the LORD delight in burnt offerings and sacrifices
 as much as in obeying the LORD?
To obey is better than sacrifice,
 and to heed is better than the fat of rams.
For rebellion is like the sin of divination,
 and arrogance like the evil of idolatry.
Because you have rejected the word of the LORD,
 he has rejected you as king. (1 Samuel 15:22–23)

No one can lead as God intended while rejecting the authority of God's Spirit. The final chapter of 1 Samuel tells us the end of Saul, a leader by the flesh. Near the end of Saul's life, he mentally and spiritually disintegrated. He gave himself over to witchcraft, which is forbidden by God. He asked the witch of Endor to summon the spirit of Samuel, and the spirit of Samuel predicted Saul's doom on the battlefield the next day.

True to the prophecy, Saul and his son Jonathan both died that day. So Saul passed out of history and into eternity—a rebellious and self-willed leader whose opportunities and second chances were wasted. It's an instructive lesson for us all.

"Evildoers foster rebellion against God; the messenger of death will be sent against them." —PROVERBS 17:11

"God sets the lonely in families, he leads out the prisoners with singing; but the rebellious live in a sun-scorched land."

—PSALM 68:6

FOR FURTHER REFLECTION:

1. What questions do you have about King Saul as a leader? How do you suppose God would answer those questions?

2. As a leader or mentor, what tempts you to "obey God halfway"? Why?

3. "The Spirit-controlled mind does not obey halfway." How does this work in real-life leadership? Explain it as if to a child.

4. What steps can you take this week to be more honest with yourself and obedient toward God in the way you lead?

16

The Leader of Faith

---

1 Samuel 16–2 Samuel 5

IN 1464, ITALIAN SCULPTOR AGOSTINO DI DUCCIO WAS commissioned by the Cathedral of Florence to create a large white marble statue. Agostino worked on the project for months but quit in frustration, saying there were too many imperfections in the marble. In 1475, sculptor Antonio Rossellino attempted to complete the project, but also quit because of the imperfections in the marble. The chisel-damaged stone remained in a storage yard for more than twenty-five years.

Finally, in 1501, a twenty-six-year-old sculptor, Michelangelo di Lodovico Buonarroti Simoni, accepted the challenge that other sculptors had rejected. The vestry board of the Cathedral told him to create a statue of the biblical hero David in his confrontation with Goliath.

Other artists of that era portrayed David after his victory, holding the severed head of Goliath. Michelangelo decided on a new approach. He depicted David before the battle, a sling in one hand, eyes alert in concentration, the veins in his neck showing a strong pulse, his body confidently posed. Michelangelo's

David is powerful and ready for battle because of his unwavering faith in God.

Michelangelo worked every day on the marble block in an outdoor courtyard. He worked nights by torchlight. He slept at odd hours with his clothes and boots on, taking Spartan meals once or twice a day. In January 1504, he unveiled the statue to the vestry board. The awed board members considered it too beautiful to place in a dark cathedral. The church gave the statue to the city of Florence, which prominently displayed Michelangelo's *David* in the sunlight of the Piazza della Signoria.

The stone block that two previous sculptors rejected is Michelangelo's masterpiece—perhaps the most breathtaking "salvage job" in history. The sculpture symbolizes the story of David himself—a shepherd boy who was rejected by men as too young, too imperfect to be a warrior or a king. God, the Master Sculptor, took the raw material of David's life and shaped him into a warrior-king of legendary proportions.

We can learn powerful leadership lessons from the story of David—his selection, anointing, rejection, exile, return, moral failure, and redemption. If you don't see yourself as a natural leader, let David be your role model.

He was the youngest of eight sons of Jesse, the one who seemed least likely to lead. Samuel examined David's seven older brothers and each of them looked like a leader. But God put His seal upon the youngest and scrawniest of the lot. God didn't look on the outward appearances. He looked at David's heart and saw the makings of a godly leader.

The apostle Paul affirmed the godly heart of David in Acts 13:22, "After removing Saul, he made David their king. God testified concerning him: 'I have found David son of Jesse, a man after my own heart; he will do everything I want him to do.'"

David was seventeen when Samuel anointed him to be Israel's future king. It was a private ceremony in David's hometown of Bethlehem, with only his father and brothers present. David was not publicly anointed King of Judah, the southern kingdom, until thirteen years later, when he was thirty. The public anointing took place in Judah's capital city, Hebron. A third anointing took place in Hebron when David was thirty-seven, and he became king of the northern kingdom as well.

How did David spend the thirteen years between his first anointing in Bethlehem and his public anointing in Hebron? He served an apprenticeship under King Saul. He befriended Saul's son Jonathan. He went through trials of adversity and testing. He lived by the Spirit, not the flesh; 1 Samuel 16:13 tells us that after Samuel first anointed David, "from that day on the Spirit of the LORD came powerfully upon David."

David spent thirteen years in obscurity. God often takes young leaders through lengthy times of obscurity and testing before he elevates them to prominence. Adversity teaches us humility, faith, and perseverance. Adversity teaches us that we can only lead effectively if we remain dependent on the power of God.

The most famous test of David's faith came when he confronted Goliath. Israel was gripped by fear as Goliath paraded up and down, taunting the Israelites. When young David came to bring food to his brothers, he found the camp of Israel in gloom and despair—and he volunteered to go out and fight Goliath.

David refused the heavy armor Saul offered him. He would face Goliath by faith alone. He took with him a leather sling and five smooth stones—and the indwelling Spirit of God. Because he went to meet Goliath in the power of the Spirit, one stone was sufficient. When David launched the stone from his sling, Goliath fell dead with the stone buried in his forehead.

A more perilous test of David's character was King Saul's jealousy of David. From 1 Samuel 18 on, we see that Saul persecuted David and tried to kill him. Saul's rage drove David into exile. During this time, David wrote many of the psalms that speak of God's faithfulness in times of adversity. Twice during this exile period, David had the opportunity to kill Saul—but he spared King Saul both times.

The story of David continues in the second book of Samuel. In 2 Samuel 1, David learned of the death of King Saul and Jonathan. Though Saul had persecuted him, David was grief-stricken over the death of Saul and Jonathan.

The death of King Saul left David free to accept the crown. Saul's death symbolizes for us the time when we first encountered the full impact of the cross of Christ. The cross ends the reign of the flesh in our lives, as symbolized by Saul, the man of the flesh. When we realize that God seeks to crucify the flesh and raise us to eternal life with Christ, we can say, "My 'inner Saul' is dead. Like David, I'm free to reign over my own life by the power of God."

At age thirty, David was anointed king over his own tribe, Judah. For seven years he ruled in the city of Hebron. While he was king over Judah, a fierce struggle raged between the house of David and the house of Saul. The old flesh dies hard. It doesn't give up easily.

Finally, in 2 Samuel 5, David captured the Jebusite fortress of Zion, in the city of Jerusalem. Zion became the City of David, and David was anointed king over a united Israel. David's victory represents the triumph of the leader of faith, the leader who is led by the Spirit of God. David is an inspiring and instructive leadership example for your life and mine.

"For it is we who are the circumcision, we who serve God by his Spirit, who boast in Christ Jesus, and who put no confidence in the flesh." —PHILIPPIANS 3:3

FOR FURTHER REFLECTION:

1. How does your own path to leadership compare to King David's journey?

2. Why do you suppose God made David wait twenty years— and fight many wars—before making it possible for him to rule a united Israel?

3. What "Goliath-sized" obstacles do you face as a leader or mentor? What do you think David would say to you about them?

4. What's one principle from the life of David that might help you lead others in God's power this week?

17

The Leader Who Fails

---

2 Samuel 6

A YOUNG LEADER ONCE EXPRESSED TO ME HIS DEEP RESENT-ment toward God. He was convinced that God had called him to carry out a certain plan. He even announced to his friends what God was about to accomplish through his leadership. Then everything fell apart—and this young leader was left feeling humiliated and angry with God.

"I can't help feeling God is unfair," he told me. "He let me down. He doesn't keep His promises."

As we talked, it became clear that this young leader had made some errors that King David also made. Both leaders—King David and my young friend—had been presumptuous about God's will and tried to carry out God's plan in their own way instead of God's way. King David learned this lesson through tragedy—and he discovered that God never compromises His commands.

In 2 Samuel 5, David became king over the unified northern and southern kingdoms of Israel and king over all twelve tribes. In 2 Samuel 6, David's first concern was to bring the Ark of God back to the center of Israel's national life. He wanted the presence of God and the holiness of God to have first place in the life of the nation.

King David's realization is much like the realization a committed Christian comes to upon recognizing that Jesus has the right to be Lord over every area of life. At that point, many Christians experience a zeal and an excitement to honor and serve God. These are the emotions that gripped David at that time, and his emotions were focused on the Ark of God.

Also known as the Ark of the Covenant, the Ark was an acacia-wood chest covered in gold, containing the two stone tablets of the Ten Commandments, Aaron's rod, and a bowl of manna—the bread from heaven that fed the Israelites as they wandered in the desert. The Ark was to be carried by staves (long wooden rods) on the shoulders of the Kohathites of the tribe of Levi. The Ark was to remain hidden beneath a covering of skins and cloth, concealed from the eyes of both the priests and the people.

At one time, the elders of Israel had taken the Ark onto the battlefield to aid them in war against the Philistines. The Philistines killed 30,000 Israelite soldiers and captured the Ark. Possession of the Ark caused the Philistines to be cursed with plagues, and they returned it to the Israelites after holding it for seven months. The Israelites took the Ark to the hilltop house of Abinadab in the town of Kiriath Jearim, about seven miles west of Jerusalem (see 1 Samuel 6:21–7:2). There it had remained for twenty years.

Now David wanted to bring the Ark to Jerusalem, so he ordered that a brand-new oxcart be built and he set the Ark in the middle of it. Then he started back toward Jerusalem, leading a procession of people who celebrated and rejoiced around the Ark.

But then the oxen stumbled in the road and the oxcart shook. A man named Uzzah, who walked alongside the cart, reached out to steady the Ark. The moment his hand touched the Ark, the awesome power of God struck Uzzah—and he fell dead.

Instantly, joy turned to tragedy and mourning. Even King David was afraid of God because of this sudden judgment against Uzzah. Why did Uzzah die? His intentions were good, as were King David's. Uzzah wanted to keep the Ark from falling to the ground—but King David had ignored God's instructions on how the ark was to be moved.

David stopped the procession and placed the Ark in the first house that was handy. Then he went back to Jerusalem, feeling bitter and resentful toward the Lord. This was the first lesson David had to learn as king. It wasn't God's fault that Uzzah died—it was David's fault.

In the Law of Moses, God gave instructions that only the Kohathites of the tribe of Levi were to be in charge of the Ark. They were to carry the Ark on poles over their shoulders (see Deuteronomy 10:8; Numbers 7:9). The Ark was not to be carried by cart or pack animals. No one was allowed to touch the Ark, not even the Kohathites (see Numbers 4:15).

David acted presumptuously. He had assumed that God would allow him to ignore the Law of Moses. He had conveyed the Ark on an oxcart in violation of God's Law—and an innocent man had died. David had to learn that God must be served God's way, not our way. Good intentions are not enough. Only obedience is sufficient to accomplish God's will.

There was nothing wrong with David's intentions, but it has been said that the road to hell is paved with good intentions. If we truly want to serve God, we must obey His commands fully and explicitly. Our good intentions cannot excuse our disobedience. We must sign on to His agenda and use His methods. Expecting Him to rubberstamp our plans is a prescription for disaster—and sometimes even death.

"There is a way that appears to be right, but in the end it leads to death." —PROVERBS 14:12

"Enter through the narrow gate. For wide is the gate and broad is the road that leads to destruction, and many enter through it." —MATTHEW 7:13

FOR FURTHER REFLECTION:

1. When has it seemed to you that God's actions were unfair? Describe that situation.

2. What's the difference between leading in obedience to God and leading with presumption toward God?

3. What does David's experience with the Ark of the Covenant say to you about the responsibility of leadership?

4. What is the prayer you can pray tomorrow morning that will help you avoid making leadership mistakes similar to those of David?

18

The Leader Who Falls

---

2 Samuel 11–12

A NUMBER OF YEARS AGO, A NATIONALLY PROMINENT pastor and conference speaker publicly confessed that he'd had an adulterous affair. Years before that confession, he had ended the affair and left the pulpit to serve as the leader of a Christian ministry. He had hoped his sin would never become public.

But after receiving an unsigned letter threatening to reveal his sin, he decided to admit everything. He resigned from the Christian organization and went back to the church he had previously pastored. He returned not as a pastor but as a member of the congregation—he believed his sin disqualified him from serving in the pulpit. He confessed his sin before the church and asked the elders to hold him accountable.

Overnight, he went from being one of the most respected Christian leaders in America to being stripped of his reputation. He underwent a lengthy period of marital therapy and spiritual discipline, seeking to restore his broken relationship with his wife, his family, and fellow believers. He later said, "I know what it is like to live with a secret. And I know what it is like to live once again in the light."[1]

He wrote a book called *Rebuilding Your Broken World*. In the book, he tells of being asked by a church in a distant city to give a talk about his moral fall and recovery. He wrote:

> When the service began, a group of young men and women took places at the front of the congregation and began to lead with instruments and voices in a chain of songs and hymns: some contemporary, others centuries old. . . I was being strangely lifted by the music and its content of thankfulness and celebration. If my heart had been heavy, the hearts of others about me were apparently light because, together, we seemed to rise in spirit . . .
>
> It was a day I shall never forget. No one in that sanctuary knew how high they had lifted one troubled man far above his broken-world anguish. Were there others there that day feeling as I did? Perhaps they would have affirmed as I did: *God was there*.[2]

In 2 Samuel 11, we come to another tragic chapter in the life of King David. The story begins with these words: "In the spring, at the time when kings go off to war . . ." In those days, kings waited for good weather before sending their armies out to the battlefield. God had called Israel to fight the idolatrous nations—nations that fed innocent children to the furnaces of brass idols.

King David usually rode at the forefront of his army—but not this year. Samuel tells us: "David sent Joab out with the king's men and the whole Israelite army. They destroyed the Ammonites and besieged Rabbah. But David remained in Jerusalem" (2 Samuel 11:1).

Here we see the beginning of David's failure. He was derelict in his duty. Whenever we are not doing what God has called us to do, we expose ourselves to temptation. David's dereliction set the stage for what came next:

One evening David got up from his bed and walked around on the roof of the palace. From the roof he saw a woman bathing. The woman was very beautiful, and David sent someone to find out about her. The man said, "She is Bathsheba, the daughter of Eliam and the wife of Uriah the Hittite." Then David sent messengers to get her. She came to him, and he slept with her. (Now she was purifying herself from her monthly uncleanness.) Then she went back home. The woman conceived and sent word to David, saying, "I am pregnant." (2 Samuel 11:2–5)

Walking on the roof of his house he saw a beautiful woman taking a bath. He sent a messenger and he inquired about her—then he took her. That is how temptation progresses. It follows the same pattern in your life and mine. Temptation starts first with a look and a desire. It's not sinful to be tempted. Desire is awakened in us simply because we are human. But if we don't deal with temptation *the moment it arises*, it will turn into sin.

So King David—the man after God's own heart—became an adulterer. Then, instead of confessing his sin and repenting of it, he committed another sin to cover it up. He brought Bathsheba's husband, Uriah, home from the battlefield and tried to trick Uriah into having sexual relations with Bathsheba. If his plan had worked, Bathsheba would have had the baby and Uriah would think the baby was his.

But Uriah, out of intense loyalty to his king and faithfulness to God, refused to spend the night with his own wife while his soldiers were out on the battlefield. David's deception failed.

In desperation, David plunged more deeply into the spiral of sin. He arranged for Uriah to be betrayed on the battlefield. He ordered his own soldiers to withdraw from Uriah in battle, allowing him to be killed by the enemy. It was one of the most callous and dishonorable acts a king could commit against a loyal soldier. David even corrupted one of his generals, making Joab a co-conspirator in the plot.

God's verdict is recorded in 2 Samuel 11:27: "The thing David had done displeased the LORD." David was an adulterer, a liar, a conspirator, and a murderer.

So God sent Nathan the prophet, who went to David and told a parable about a rich man with many flocks of sheep who took away a poor man's ewe lamb. Hearing the story, David angrily said, "The man who did this must die!" (2 Samuel 12:1–5).

Nathan said, "You are the man!"

Horrified, David realized that the story was about his sin with Bathsheba. The cover-up was over. He confessed his sin and repented. He later wrote Psalm 51, a psalm of confession and repentance. If you are ever burdened by guilt and shame, pray the words of Psalm 51.

God's grace and forgiveness are so great that He will even restore the person who has committed such sins as these. But even though God's forgiveness is all-encompassing, sin still has natural consequences. Nathan told David that the sword would never depart from his house because of his sin. The prophecy was fulfilled when Absalom, David's own son, rose up against him.

Though the law demands death for the sin of murder, God in His grace forgave and restored David after his confession. But David was plagued by the natural consequences of his sin for the rest of his life. As the New Testament tells us, "Do not be deceived"—that is, don't kid yourself—"God cannot be mocked. A man reaps what he sows. Whoever sows to please their flesh, from the flesh will reap destruction" (Galatians 6:7–8).

From beginning to end, the life of King David is rich in

lessons for leaders. David was a leader of great faith, a man after God's own heart—but also a leader who sinned greatly and paid a great price for his moral failure. His life is a lesson and a warning to us. May we always emulate his faith—and may we always be warned by his great failure.

"No temptation has overtaken you except what is common to mankind. And God is faithful; he will not let you be tempted beyond what you can bear. But when you are tempted, he will also provide a way out so that you can endure it."

—1 CORINTHIANS 10:13

FOR FURTHER REFLECTION:

1. What's your initial reaction to the facts of David's affair with Bathsheba, and his subsequent sins?

2. What makes you any different from King David? Explain.

3. In your opinion, what's the best way to guard against the temptations a leader is likely to face? And what's the best approach after failure has occurred? Defend your answers.

4. How might Psalm 51 be helpful to you as you lead or mentor others this week?

19

The Introspective Leader

Proverbs 20:27; Psalm 51

WE ONCE HELD A NEW YEAR'S EVE WATCHNIGHT SERVICE
at Peninsula Bible Church. I stood on the platform with a candle in my hand, the only light in the room. I shared a verse from
Proverbs: "The spirit of man is the candle of the LORD, searching all the inward parts of the heart" (Proverbs 20:27 MEV).

I had prepared a devotional, but as I looked at the congregation in the dim light of that candle, I felt God leading me to
simply speak from my heart.

"When I was a young Christian," I said, "I thought I was
a pretty good person—God only had to sand off a few rough
edges and I'd be nearly perfect. In these moments, the Lord
has brought to mind the flaws and sins He has revealed to me
over the years—selfish actions, hurtful things I've done and said,
outbursts of anger.

"Every time I've plumbed new depths of my own sinful-
ness, I've also experienced new depths of God's cleansing power.
While my self-esteem has sunk lower over the years, my sense of
God's forgiveness has soared higher. I increasingly find myself
praying the words of the Psalmist: 'Search me, God, and know

my heart; test me and know my anxious thoughts. See if there is any offensive way in me, and lead me in the way everlasting'" (Psalm 139:23–24).

After I spoke, others shared. We had a beautiful time, singing songs and praising God together, praying and opening our hearts to one another. I was glad I listened to God's prompting, and glad that my own spirit, like a candle of the Lord, went searching through my memories, revealing God's forgiving grace in my life.

In the life of a godly leader, honest introspection leads to an awareness of sin, the confession of guilt, and a plea for cleansing and forgiveness. We see this in Psalm 51, which David composed after his sin with Bathsheba:

> Have mercy on me, O God,
>   according to your unfailing love;
> according to your great compassion
>   blot out my transgressions.
> Wash away all my iniquity
>   and cleanse me from my sin. (Psalm 51:1–2)

David asks for three things: mercy ("Have mercy on me, O God"), a fresh start ("According to your great compassion blot out my transgressions"), and cleansing ("Wash away all my iniquity and cleanse me from my sin"). David stands before the Almighty Judge as a condemned criminal—and criminals don't want justice, they want mercy. David knows his debt of sin can never be repaid—he stands bankrupt before God. His soul is indelibly stained by sin, and only God can cleanse him. He declares:

> For I know my transgressions,
>   and my sin is always before me.

> Against you, you only, have I sinned
>> and done what is evil in your sight;
> so you are right in your verdict
>> and justified when you judge. (Psalm 51:3–4)

This is an amazing statement: "Against you, you only, have I sinned." Why does David say that his sin is against God alone? He seduced Bathsheba and destroyed her marriage. He murdered her husband Uriah, that loyal servant from the land of the Hittites who chose Israel's God as his God. David made Joab a co-conspirator in Uriah's murder. But David is not downplaying the harm he caused others. He is acknowledging that he harmed his relationship with God far more.

The closing verses of Psalm 51 contain eight principles for safeguarding our hearts against sin:

First, pray for wisdom and understanding in the deepest places of your heart. David wrote, "You taught me wisdom in that secret place" (verse 6). We fool ourselves into thinking, "It's only a minor sin," or, "I'm not really hurting anyone." Pray, "Lord teach me wisdom to understand reality, so I won't sin against you."

Second, pray for the cleansing of guilt through the sacrifice of Christ. David wrote, "Cleanse me with hyssop, and I will be clean" (verse 7). At the first Passover in Egypt, God told the Hebrew people to stain their doorframes with lamb's blood, using a sponge-like plant called hyssop. The blood-stained doorframes symbolize the blood of Jesus on the cross.

Third, pray for the joy that comes with forgiveness. David wrote, "Let me hear joy and gladness; let the bones you have crushed rejoice" (verse 8). Ask God to lift the bone-crushing weight of guilt from your soul and give you joy that will enable you to resist temptation.

Fourth, pray that God would blot your sin out of His sight. David wrote, "Hide your face from my sins and blot out all my iniquity" (verse 9). God promises to answer this prayer and remove our guilt.

Fifth, ask God to renew a pure and upright spirit within you. David wrote, "Create in me a pure heart, O God, and renew a steadfast spirit within me" (verse 10). David knew that his old heart must be put to death. He prayed for a steadfast spirit to stand firm against sin.

Sixth, pray for the presence of the Holy Spirit to guide, comfort, and strengthen you. David wrote, "Do not . . . take your Holy Spirit from me" (verse 11). There is no stronger safeguard against sin than God's indwelling Spirit.

Seventh, pray for a renewed sense of what it means to be saved. David wrote, "Restore to me the joy of your salvation" (verse 12). Salvation means so much more than eternal life in heaven. We are saved from sin to live righteous lives in the here and now.

Eighth, pray for a willing spirit. David wrote, "And grant me a willing spirit, to sustain me" (verse 12). To keep from falling back into old sins, we must replace our old sinful heart with a spirit that eagerly wants to do God's will. We will struggle and fail at times, but we will be empowered to resist temptation if we are worshipping, praising, praying, witnessing, and serving others.

Once, when I was preparing to preach on Psalm 51, I received an anonymous letter from a man engaged in serious ongoing sin. He said, "I don't think God will judge me for my sin, because He hasn't given me the power to break this habit."

That Sunday, I read the letter before the congregation, then said, "This man is self-deceived. God *has* given us the power to live victoriously over sin. David wrote, 'Grant me a willing spirit, to sustain me.' If that is our sincere prayer, God *will* grant us a willing spirit."

The man wrote me again, saying, "You were right, Pastor. God *does* grant us a willing spirit if we sincerely ask Him. Psalm 51 is now the daily prayer of my heart."

If you struggle with sin, may this psalm be the prayer of your heart.

> *"His divine power has given us everything we need for a godly life through our knowledge of him who called us by his own glory and goodness."* —2 PETER 1:3

FOR FURTHER REFLECTION:

1. Use any situation that comes to mind right now and finish this sentence: "If I had it to do over, here's what I'd do differently . . ."

2. "Search me, God, and know my heart" (Psalm 139:23). What actually happens when a leader prays that prayer? Explain.

3. Of the eight principles for safeguarding our hearts against sin (from Psalm 51), which do you find most helpful? Why?

4. Taking into account what you've learned about being an introspective leader, what challenge would you give yourself to pursue each day this week? Write it down.

20

The Psalm of
a Godly Leader

Psalm 20

AN AIRLINE FLIGHT ATTENDANT IS A LEADER. THE FIRST duty of a flight attendant is passenger safety. Attendants are trained to give first aid, administer CPR, and deal with aggressive or intoxicated passengers. In an emergency—a fire, crash landing, or hijacking—flight attendants take charge, give orders, and direct passengers to safety. Though flight attendants are leaders, they rarely get the respect they deserve.

I spoke at a conference of the Fellowship of Christian Airline Personnel in Chattanooga. During the conference, a flight attendant told me of an incident during a recent flight. She was in the aisle, serving coffee, when a male passenger touched her in a sexual way. She pushed his hand away and continued on, feeling angry and humiliated.

She silently asked God for wisdom, and the words of 1 Corinthians 3:17 came to her mind: "If anyone destroys God's temple, God will destroy that person; for God's temple is sacred . . ."

She went back to the man and said, "What you did was unacceptable. My life belongs to Jesus Christ and my body is the temple of the Holy Spirit. The Bible says that God will destroy anyone who damages His temple."

The man stammered, "Don't say any more. It'll never happen again."

Walking away, she thanked God for removing her humiliation and placing the shame where it belonged—on the offender. She conducted herself as a godly leader.

Psalm 20 is the psalm of the godly leader—a prayer of the people of Israel for their king as he goes to war:

> May the LORD answer you when you are in distress;
>   may the name of the God of Jacob protect you.
> May he send you help from the sanctuary
>   and grant you support from Zion. (Psalm 20:1–2)

This psalm acknowledges that to be a leader is to know distress. Every leader has enemies and fights battles, whether on the battlefield, in the office, or in the home. As leaders, we cannot escape trials. We face them in God's strength, with His sword in our fists, battling our way to victory.

How does God give us victory over trials and adversaries? He sends us "help from the sanctuary." In the Old Testament, "the sanctuary" is a picture of the place where we meet with God. In Israel it was the Temple, where the Israelites gathered to hear the Word of God. In Psalm 73, the psalm writer Asaph wrote that he envied the wealth of the wicked until he "entered the sanctuary of God; then I understood their final destiny" (Psalm 73:17). In the sanctuary, he gained God's view of reality.

What is this sanctuary? A church building, made of stone? No. God's sanctuary is a storehouse of truth where we gain wisdom and understanding. The sanctuary of God is the Bible. In the sanctuary of God's Word, we find help for every leadership challenge we face.

Our twenty-sixth president, Woodrow Wilson, was a man of faith. He led our nation through World War I and helped create the League of Nations, the forerunner of the United Nations. He said, "The Bible is the word of life . . . When you have read the Bible you will know that it is the Word of God, because you will have found it the key to your own heart, your own happiness, and your own duty."[1]

The psalmist reveals the extent to which God's help is available for the battles of life:

> May he remember all your sacrifices
> and accept your burnt offerings.
> May he give you the desire of your heart
> and make all your plans succeed.
> May we shout for joy over your victory
> and lift up our banners in the name of our God.
> May the LORD grant all your requests. (Psalm 20:3–5)

What is the deepest desire of your heart? A new car, a new house, a fat bank account? These "wants" are not your deepest desire. What you truly desire is to be a joyful, whole human being. You want to be a confident, courageous, faithful leader, ready to do God's will and influence others for Him.

The good news of Psalm 20 is that God has promised to grant you the desire of your heart. He has promised to fulfill your God-inspired plans. He has promised to give you victory in the battles you face.

Does God truly promise to make our plans succeed? Yes—if our hearts are aligned with His. If we desire what He desires for our lives, then our plans will be God's plans, our desires will be His desires—and He will make our plans succeed.

The psalmist reminds us that victory in battle leads to rejoicing. We shout for joy and lift our banners as we celebrate the triumphant name of our God. The psalmist pictures a great gathering of victorious believers. Victory is never a solitary accomplishment—especially for leaders. When you experience victory as a leader, you share the joy with the people you have inspired, supported, motivated, and encouraged. Raise a banner together in God's name.

Your family devotions should be a celebration of victory. Your worship services and business meetings should be celebrations of victory. Your home Bible study should be a celebration of victory.

In verses 6 through 8, the godly leader responds to the prayer of the people with a statement that is full of confidence and faith:

> Now this I know:
>   The LORD gives victory to his anointed.
> He answers him from his heavenly sanctuary
>   with the victorious power of his right hand.
> Some trust in chariots and some in horses,
>   but we trust in the name of the LORD our God.
> They are brought to their knees and fall,
>   but we rise up and stand firm. (Psalm 20:6–8)

My definition of a Christian—and especially a Christian leader—is "a person who is completely fearless, continually cheerful, and constantly in trouble." Godly leaders face hard decisions, turbulent circumstances, and fierce adversaries.

We may not always be victorious as the world defines victory. God may not always deliver us from enemies, pain, tragedy, or death. God's chosen form of victory may not always look like victory from a human perspective. Some of the greatest victories for God have been won by those who were martyred for their faith.

The godly leader doesn't trust in earthly armament and weaponry, but in the name of the Lord. That's where our hope and confidence lie.

Next, the king's followers respond:

> LORD, give victory to the king!
> Answer us when we call! (Psalm 20:9)

The people will pray for their leader, and God will give him the victory. You and I don't know what battles lie ahead, but God knows. He will grant us victory both in life and in death. We will shout for joy and raise our banners high, because the Lord of Glory is with us.

"I have told you these things, so that in me you may have peace. In this world you will have trouble. But take heart! I have overcome the world." —JOHN 16:33

Ray Stedman on Leadership

FOR FURTHER REFLECTION:

1. "A person who is completely fearless, continually cheerful, and constantly in trouble." In your experience, how have you seen this definition of a leader in action? Describe it.

2. How exactly does a Christian leader find "sanctuary" in the Bible? Explain it as if speaking to someone who has never seen a Bible.

3. For the Psalmist, success was victory in war. How do you define your success as a leader? Why?

4. What steps can you take this week to gain more insight into God's perspective on victory and defeat?

—108—

21

The Leader
Falsely Accused

Psalm 109

I RECEIVED A CALL FROM A YOUNG PASTOR IN ANOTHER church. He told me his secretary had become angry with him over an administrative matter, so she had forged a letter and claimed he had written it. The letter portrayed him as a vile and immoral person. She presented the letter to the elders as evidence of the pastor's wrongdoing.

The elders accepted the letter as proof, in violation of God's Word. Paul, in 1 Timothy 5:19, wrote, "Do not entertain an accusation against an elder unless it is brought by two or three witnesses." Though the pastor denied writing the letter, the elders had taken the word of the secretary and fired him.

"The elders have put the burden of proof on me," he told me. "I'm presumed guilty and I can't prove I didn't write that letter."

Weeks passed. The secretary, suffering pangs of conscience, went to the elders and confessed she had written the letter herself. The pastor was restored to his position, and the elders made a public announcement of their error. God used the experience to teach that church about responding to accusations.

To be a leader is to be a target for attacks of all kinds. David knew the pain of being falsely accused, and he poured his feelings into the words of Psalm 109. We don't know for sure, but David may have written this psalm after the events recorded in 1 Samuel 25.

Before David became King of Israel, King Saul hunted him and tried to kill him. David was on the run, hiding in the desert with his loyal men. During their exile, David and his men aided people, protecting them from bandits. One man they helped was a wealthy rancher named Nabal.

After weeks in the desert, David and his men ran low on provisions, so he sent ten of his men to Nabal, asking for any food the rancher could spare. Nabal responded with a torrent of insults against David and he sent the men away empty-handed. In response, David decided to attack the ranch and kill Nabal. When Nabal's wife Abigail heard that her husband had insulted David, she and her servants took bread, wine, and meat to David's camp and begged him to spare Nabal's life. Moved by her pleas, David sent Abigail home in peace.

Ten days later, God stopped Nabal's heart. When David heard that Nabal was dead, he praised God for sending Abigail to talk him out of taking revenge. God himself avenged David, and Abigail became David's wife.

In the opening lines of Psalm 109, David lays out the pain of being falsely accused:

> My God, whom I praise,
>   do not remain silent,
> for people who are wicked and deceitful
>   have opened their mouths against me;
>   they have spoken against me with lying tongues.

With words of hatred they surround me;
    they attack me without cause.
In return for my friendship they accuse me,
    but I am a man of prayer.
They repay me evil for good,
    and hatred for my friendship. (Psalm 109:1–5)

In the Sermon on the Mount, Jesus commands us to love our enemies and pray for those who persecute us. Though David's first impulse was revenge, he understood this New Testament principle of praying for one's enemies. He wrote, "In return for my friendship they accuse me, but I am a man of prayer." When falsely accused, David responded (after Abigail's persuasive appeal) as a man of prayer.

The next section of Psalm 109 has been widely misinterpreted. Many people think that these are David's words, aimed at his attackers. But David is quoting his *attackers'* insults against *him*:

Appoint someone evil to oppose my enemy;
    let an accuser stand at his right hand.
When he is tried, let him be found guilty,
    and may his prayers condemn him.
May his days be few;
    may another take his place of leadership.
May his children be fatherless
    and his wife a widow.
May his children be wandering beggars;
    may they be driven from their ruined homes.
May a creditor seize all he has;
    may strangers plunder the fruits of his labor.
May no one extend kindness to him
    or take pity on his fatherless children.

> May his descendants be cut off,
>> heir names blotted out from the next generation.
> May the iniquity of his fathers be remembered before
>> the LORD;
>> may the sin of his mother never be blotted out.
> May their sins always remain before the LORD,
>> that he may blot out their name from the earth.
>
> (Psalm 109:6–15)

The psalmist is not calling down curses on his enemies. He's *quoting* his enemies. The ancient Hebrew language did not contain quotation marks, but there's a clear distinction between David's words and his enemies' words. He spoke of his enemies in the plural: "With words of hatred *they* surround me; *they* attack me without cause." His enemies speak of him in the singular: "When *he* is tried, let *him* be found guilty, and may his prayers condemn *him*."

Verses 6 to 19 should be set in quotation marks because they are the words of his enemies. Seeing how hateful and relentless his accusers are, we understand David's suffering. This interpretation of these lines is confirmed by verse 20:

> May this be the LORD's payment to my accusers,
> to those who speak evil of me. (Psalm 109:20)

Verses 6 through 15 depict the psalmist's enemies rigging a trial and placing a false accuser at his right hand to condemn him. David's enemies aren't going to murder him in an alley. They'll assassinate his character in a courtroom and let the law do their dirty work.

They seek to destroy David and his leadership role: "May his days be few; may another take his place of leadership." They even seek to destroy his family: "May his children be fatherless

and his wife a widow. May his children be wandering beggars."
David's godless enemies want to destroy his wife and children.
They even pray for the eternal damnation of him and his family:
"May their sins always remain before the LORD." A heart full of
hate wants others to suffer eternally.

It's a dangerous thing to curse another human being. Jesus
said, "Do not judge, and you will not be judged. Do not condemn, and you will not be condemned. Forgive, and you will
be forgiven" (Luke 6:37). If we condemn others to hell for some
hurt they have caused us, how should we be judged for the hurts
we cause others?

Every leader is a target for false accusations. Even righteous
leaders make enemies. When falsely accused, don't give in to
hate. Love your enemies. Pray for those who persecute you. Let
God be your defender and avenger. That is the message of Psalm
109, a psalm for leaders who are falsely accused.

*"Blessed are you when people insult you, persecute you and
falsely say all kinds of evil against you because of me."*

—MATTHEW 5:11

*"Then I heard a loud voice in heaven say:
'Now have come the salvation and the power
    and the kingdom of our God,
    and the authority of his Messiah.
For the accuser of our brothers and sisters,
    who accuses them before our God day and night,
    has been hurled down.'"*

—REVELATION 12:10

FOR FURTHER REFLECTION:

1. What are your first thoughts after reading about Psalm 109 and David's encounter with Nabal?

2. What principles of leadership do you see in David's experience?

3. In your opinion, what is a leader's best defense against false accusations? Defend your answer.

4. If Abigail were to speak to you about your intentions for the week ahead, what might she say? And how might your intentions change?

22

The Temple Builder

---

2 Chronicles 1–9

I ONCE MET A PASTOR FROM ANOTHER STATE; WE'LL CALL him Pastor Brown. He had read my book *Body Life* and was incorporating some of its principles into his church. He told me another pastor had asked him, "What are you doing at your church?"

Pastor Brown replied, "We're sharing one another's burdens and meeting one another's needs. We have a service where we talk about our problems and pray for each other."

"Why do you do that?"

"Because," Pastor Brown said, "the New Testament tells us to."

"Well, you won't get anywhere with that approach."

"The Bible doesn't tell us we're supposed to 'get anywhere.' It just tells us how we're supposed to live."

"Well, I think that's a foolish way to run a church."

"Then we're fools—but we're God's fools, following God's commands, obeying God's Word. We're going to keep right on practicing this foolishness."

The church is the body of Christ and God's people are His dwelling place. As Paul wrote to the Christians in Corinth, "Don't you know that you yourselves are God's temple and that God's Spirit dwells in your midst?" (1 Corinthians 3:16).

In Old Testament times, before the Holy Spirit came to indwell the church (see Acts 2), God had a physical dwelling place among the people of Israel. From the time of Moses until the time of King David, that was a tent called the Tabernacle (in the original Hebrew, the word is *mishkan*, meaning "dwelling place").

Though the Hebrew people called the Tabernacle (and later, the Temple) the "dwelling place" of God, they didn't believe a structure could *contain* God. They understood that God is *everywhere*. As Paul told the people of Athens, "The God who made the world and everything in it . . . does not live in temples built by human hands" (Acts 17:24).

The Tabernacle and Temple were the places where the people could meet God and be restored from the effects of sin. The people could offer sacrifices, raise their voices in prayer, and confess their sins. In response, God would restore and forgive His people.

In 2 Samuel 7, after King David had built his own palace in Jerusalem, it troubled him that the "dwelling place" of God was a tent, not a permanent structure. He told the prophet Nathan, "Here I am, living in a house of cedar, while the ark of God remains in a tent." Nathan told David that if he built a permanent Temple, God would approve.

Later, however, God spoke to Nathan, saying:

> "Go and tell my servant David, 'This is what the LORD says: Are you the one to build me a house to dwell in? I have

not dwelt in a house from the day I brought the Israelites up out of Egypt to this day. I have been moving from place to place with a tent as my dwelling. Wherever I have moved with all the Israelites, did I ever say to any of their rulers whom I commanded to shepherd my people Israel, "Why have you not built me a house of cedar? . . ."

"'The LORD declares to you that the LORD himself will establish a house for you: When your days are over and you rest with your ancestors, I will raise up your offspring to succeed you, your own flesh and blood, and I will establish his kingdom. He is the one who will build a house for my Name, and I will establish the throne of his kingdom forever." (2 Samuel 7:5–7, 11–13)

Why did God reject David as the builder of His temple? God told David, "You are not to build a house for my Name, because you have shed much blood on the earth in my sight" (1 Chronicles 22:8). This didn't mean David sinned in going to war; he had fought at God's command. After David defeated the Jebusites, 1 Chronicles 11:9 records, "And David became more and more powerful, because the LORD Almighty was with him." That last phrase literally means "the Lord of Armies was with him." David was a soldier, and soldiering is a noble profession.

But God would only allow a man who symbolized Christ, the Prince of Peace, to build the Temple. God promised David that his offspring would build a house for His Name. That offspring was Solomon, whose name in Hebrew means "peaceful."

God had chosen David to symbolize Jesus, the conquering King over all. But God rejected David's plan to build the Temple and gave that honor to his son Solomon. Though disappointed, David agreed with God that the Temple should be built by his son.

Solomon was crowned King of Israel while David still lived. The first nine chapters of 2 Chronicles focus on Solomon and the Temple. The book opens with Solomon's prayer for wisdom:

> That night God appeared to Solomon and said to him, "Ask for whatever you want me to give you."
>
> Solomon answered God, "You have shown great kindness to David my father and have made me king in his place. . . . Give me wisdom and knowledge, that I may lead this people, for who is able to govern this great people of yours?"
>
> God said to Solomon, "Since this is your heart's desire and you have not asked for wealth, possessions or honor, nor for the death of your enemies, and since you have not asked for a long life but for wisdom and knowledge to govern my people over whom I have made you king, therefore wisdom and knowledge will be given you. And I will also give you wealth, possessions and honor, such as no king who was before you ever had and none after you will have." (2 Chronicles 1:7–8, 10–12)

Solomon chose a heart of wisdom rather than wealth. Under Solomon's wise leadership, Israel grew in economic power, international trade, and cultural achievements. The Temple of Solomon replaced the Tabernacle as the center of worship. This symbolizes the truth that when the Lord Jesus reigns as King in our lives, we no longer have a relationship with the Tabernacle, the impermanent tent of worship. We now walk in a permanent relationship with God. He reigns in our hearts, and the light of God's house shines in our lives.

In the New Testament, we as believers are the Temple, the dwelling place of the Lord. Just as Solomon is the builder of the Temple in Jerusalem, the Lord Jesus is the Builder of the Temple of the human spirit.

It took Solomon seven years to build the Temple—yet 1 Kings 7:1 tells us that Solomon lavished thirteen years on the construction of his palace. This suggests that Solomon was already succumbing to the lure of materialism and self-centeredness. Later in life, Solomon's many wives—700 wives of royal birth and 300 concubines—led to his downfall. His wives included Pharaoh's daughter and princesses from Ammon, Edom, Moab, and other nations. Solomon permitted them to worship false gods, and their idolatry tainted Solomon's devotion to God.

Solomon serves as an example and a warning to us as leaders. The prayer of an effective leader is, "Give me wisdom and knowledge, that I may lead this people." Stay focused on the wisdom of God throughout your life, and never let selfish desires crowd out your love of wisdom. God is building His house in you, because your life is the dwelling place of God.

"The beginning of wisdom is this: Get wisdom. Though it cost all you have, get understanding." —PROVERBS 4:7

"If any of you lacks wisdom, you should ask God, who gives generously to all without finding fault, and it will be given to you." —JAMES 1:5

FOR FURTHER REFLECTION:

1. When was a time that God, as he did with David, did not allow you to accomplish a good plan you made with intention to honor Him? What happened?

2. How does a person like you "make a house for the Lord" in the areas of leadership authority? Explain.

3. What lessons in leadership do you see in Solomon's example? Make a list.

4. Tomorrow you have a new opportunity to be a leader that God approves. So what will you do?

23

A Leader's
Responsibilities

Jeremiah 21–23

ONE OF THE MOST BRUTAL MILITARY SIEGES IN HISTORY WAS
the Babylonian siege of Jerusalem. Babylon first invaded Judah
in 605 BC, the year Nebuchadnezzar became king of Babylon.
In that invasion, Nebuchadnezzar's forces entered Jerusalem
and looted the palace of King Jehoiakim and the Temple of
Solomon. Many young princes of Judah were deported to Babylon—the first wave of deportations.

The next Babylonian invasion of Judah occurred in 597 BC,
when Jehoachin was king of Judah. The Babylonians captured
Jerusalem and forced a second deportation of Jews. Among
those deported was Jehoachin himself, who had reigned for three
months. Nebuchadnezzar installed Jehoachin's uncle, Zedekiah,
as a vassal king controlled by the Babylonian Empire.

In the ninth year of his reign, Zedekiah revolted against
Babylon and aligned himself with Nebuchadnezzar's enemy,
Pharaoh Hophra of Egypt. Enraged, Nebuchadnezzar invaded

Judah, laying siege to Jerusalem in December 589 BC. As related in 2 Kings 25, Nebuchadnezzar's forces surrounded the city. The people were driven to cannibalism by the scourge of starvation. The siege lasted thirty months and ended with the destruction of the city and the Temple in 586 BC. The Babylonians plundered the city, slaughtered most of the people, and led thousands into captivity.

One of the few survivors was the prophet Jeremiah. He had preached a message of repentance in Judah for forty years, without success. He had predicted the destruction of Jerusalem, but no one listened.

In Jeremiah 21, the prophet recalls the beginning stages of the final siege of Babylon in 589 BC. King Zedekiah was on the throne. The royal house of Israel, which began with King Saul and King David, was nearing the end. Nebuchadnezzar's army was approaching, so Zedekiah sent a panic-stricken message to Jeremiah: "Inquire now of the LORD for us because Nebuchadnezzar king of Babylon is attacking us. Perhaps the LORD will perform wonders for us as in times past so that he will withdraw from us."

After leading the nation into sin and idolatry, Zedekiah hoped that God would let bygones be bygones. But why should God work a miracle on behalf of the disobedient? He had given plenty of warnings through Jeremiah. At some point, it's time to reap what we have sown. God is gracious and patient, but He will not be mocked. To the king's dismay, Jeremiah replied that God was going to help Babylon fight *against* Judah.

Zedekiah and the elders of the nation had failed God and His people in two important leadership responsibilities. In chapter 22, Jeremiah described the responsibilities of a leader, and a leader's first responsibility is to *shepherd the flock*:

This is what the LORD says: Do what is just and right. Rescue from the hand of the oppressor the one who has been robbed. Do no wrong or violence to the foreigner, the fatherless or the widow, and do not shed innocent blood in this place. (Jeremiah 22:3)

In chapter 23, Jeremiah tells us that a leader's second responsibility is to *do no wrong*:

"Woe to the shepherds who are destroying and scattering the sheep of my pasture!" declares the LORD. Therefore this is what the LORD, the God of Israel, says to the shepherds who tend my people: "Because you have scattered my flock and driven them away and have not bestowed care on them, I will bestow punishment on you for the evil you have done," declares the LORD. (Jeremiah 23:1–2)

Throughout the Old and the New Testaments, God uses the imagery of sheep and shepherds when speaking of His concept of government. Leaders are to view themselves as shepherds of the people, watching over the people, defending their rights, and protecting them from harm.

Instead of guarding God's flock, Judah's leaders had scattered the flock. They had mistreated God's flock. They had led the nation into idolatry and apostasy while oppressing and robbing the people. They had committed violence against foreigners, denied justice to widows and orphans, and murdered the innocent.

In Romans 13, Paul states that every government leader, every elected or appointed official, is a minister of God. This is true whether that person is a believer or not, and whether that person knows it or not. It's true whether that person is a godly shepherd or an ungodly tyrant. If a leader is guilty of wrongdoing, he or she will be held accountable by God.

King Zedekiah and his cronies had become rich through corruption and oppression of the people. Now God, through the Babylonians, was presenting the bill. Jeremiah wrote:

> "Woe to him who builds his palace by unrighteousness,
>   his upper rooms by injustice,
> making his own people work for nothing,
>   not paying them for their labor.
> He says, 'I will build myself a great palace
>   with spacious upper rooms.'
> So he makes large windows in it,
>   panels it with cedar
>   and decorates it in red." (Jeremiah 22:13–14)

Throughout history, kings have always felt entitled to live like—well, like kings! They want the best of everything—the biggest homes, the grandest furnishings, gold fixtures, cedar-paneled rooms, red-velvet drapes. Even as the nation was going bankrupt, even as a hostile enemy marched toward the city gates, King Zedekiah was redecorating the palace in high style. Yet he built his palace on a foundation of unrighteousness and injustice.

Government corruption is bad enough, but when the religious leaders are corrupt as well, what hope is there for the nation? Jeremiah wrote:

> Concerning the prophets:
> My heart is broken within me;
>   all my bones tremble.
> I am like a drunken man,
>   like a strong man overcome by wine,
> because of the LORD
>   and his holy words.

The land is full of adulterers;
>> because of the curse the land lies parched
>> and the pastures in the wilderness are withered.
The prophets follow an evil course
>> and use their power unjustly. (Jeremiah 23:9–10)

Behind the king stands the prophet. When the heart of the king goes astray, the religious leader must confront the king. But if the heart of the prophet is evil, there is no one to hold the king accountable—and there is no hope for the people. The prophets of Judah preached pious platitudes, claiming everything was going to work out. There was no need for confession of sin, no need for national repentance. The prophets filled the people with false hope.

Meanwhile, the Babylonians were coming to shatter the walls and drench the streets with blood. Soon the air would ring with the screams of the dying and the wailing of mourners.

Leaders at every level—in the family, in the church, in organizations and corporations, in schools, in the government—have a dual obligation: shepherd the flock and do no wrong. That is the message of Jeremiah.

"But select capable men from all the people—men who fear God, trustworthy men who hate dishonest gain—and appoint them as officials over thousands, hundreds, fifties and tens."
—EXODUS 18:21

"Kings detest wrongdoing, for a throne is established through righteousness."
—PROVERBS 16:12

FOR FURTHER REFLECTION:

1. In your opinion, was Jeremiah a success or a failure as a leader? Explain your answer.

2. In your role as a leader or mentor, what does it mean to shepherd your flock? To do no wrong?

3. Assume that you are in the symbolic role of a "king" in your area of leadership. Who is the "prophet" that stands behind you? How do you interact with that person?

4. As you look at Zedekiah, what truths about leadership do you see? How will you apply those truths this week?

24

A Leader among the Lions

Daniel 1–6

A YOUNG BUSINESSMAN ATTENDED OUR CHURCH FOR SEV-
eral months, then stopped coming. I called him and asked,
"Why have you stopped attending church?"

"I hesitate to come anymore. I feel like a hypocrite. When
I'm at work, I can't seem to live like a Christian. I lose my temper, I swear, I treat my coworkers badly. Sitting in church, I feel
like I'm living a lie."

"A hypocrite," I said, "is someone who acts like something he
isn't. When you come to church, are you acting like a Christian
or a non-Christian?"

"At church, I act like a Christian."

"Are you a Christian?"

"Yes, I am."

"All right, then. If you're a Christian, then when are you
acting like one?"

"When I'm at church."

"And when are you acting like someone you aren't?"

"Oh, I see what you mean. I'm being a hypocrite at work!"

"Exactly. The only time you aren't a hypocrite is when you come to church. So don't stop coming to church. Instead, stop being a hypocrite at work."

With that new perspective, he went back into the business world, daily asking God for the strength to live like a Christian seven days a week. If you don't want to be a hypocrite, don't give up your worship and fellowship with other believers. Give up your worldliness. Be a bold witness and a Christian leader every day of the week.

If you want a role model of consistent godly leadership in a godless world, study the life of Daniel. Throughout his adult life, he was a leader, serving in the Babylon and Persian Empires. How did this young Jewish leader end up in Babylon and Persia?

In 599 BC, King Nebuchadnezzar of Babylon laid siege to Jerusalem, conquered the kingdom of Judah, and took the Jewish people captive. Among the captives were four young men from Jerusalem's most influential families—Daniel, Hananiah, Mishael, and Azariah. The Babylonians renamed them Belteshazzar, Shadrach, Meshach, and Abednego.

These young Jewish men learned the language, traditions, and literature of the Babylonians. After three years of training, they were expected to serve in King Nebuchadnezzar's court. But the Babylonians demanded that the four Jewish scholars eat foods that God had told them not to eat. The Babylonians viewed their refusal to eat the king's food as an insult to King Nebuchadnezzar.

The cruelty of Nebuchadnezzar was legendary. During the conquest of Jerusalem, Nebuchadnezzar executed the sons of King Zedekiah in front of him, then had Zedekiah's eyes put out so that the last thing he ever saw was the death of his sons. Nebuchadnezzar also roasted two false prophets to death over a fire (see Jeremiah 29:21–22).

These four young Hebrews risked torture and death to stand on their principles. Though the Babylonians threatened them, they refused the meat of the king's table and asked to eat only vegetables. After ten days on this diet, they were healthier than the Babylonians who ate the royal meat. The Babylonians exalted Daniel and his friends and gave them positions of importance in the land of their captivity. But their peril was far from over.

In Daniel 3, Daniel's three Hebrew companions, Shadrach, Meshach, and Abednego, faced another life-and-death challenge. King Nebuchadnezzar erected a statue of himself and issued an edict that everyone in the kingdom should worship the image or be executed. When the Babylonian call to worship sounded, all of Babylon worshipped the image—except Shadrach, Meshach, and Abednego.

Daniel 3:8 tells us that "some astrologers came forward and denounced the Jews" for disobeying the king's edict. Enraged, King Nebuchadnezzar condemned the three men to death in a fiery furnace. Though the three Hebrews expected God to rescue them, they were ready to accept a fiery death rather than worship the image. God honored their faith by taking them safely through the furnace. As a result, King Nebuchadnezzar was moved to worship God, and he promoted all three to positions of greater responsibility.

Why wasn't Daniel condemned to the furnace with his three friends? He undoubtedly defied the king's edict as they did, but he served the king in a different governmental capacity than his three friends. The Babylonian royal court employed astrologers, mages, sorcerers, and religious scholars from many conquered nations. Shadrach, Meshach, and Abednego were spokesmen for the God of the Jews. The astrologers hated the Hebrews and their God, so they accused the three Hebrew scholars, but probably had no contact with Daniel.

In Daniel 6, however, we find that Daniel made political enemies of his own. By that time, the Persian Empire had conquered the Babylonian Empire. Daniel served the court of the Persian emperor, Darius the Mede. The Bible tells us, "Now Daniel so distinguished himself among the administrators and the satraps by his exceptional qualities that the king planned to set him over the whole kingdom. At this, the administrators and the satraps tried to find grounds for charges against Daniel in his conduct of government affairs, but they were unable to do so" (Daniel 6:3–4).

Just as the jealous astrologers had tried to destroy Daniel's three friends, Daniel's political enemies wanted to destroy him. They maneuvered King Darius into issuing a decree forbidding anyone to pray to any god or king but Darius. They knew Daniel would disobey the decree. In fact, Daniel went out of his way to be "caught" praying, because he prayed three times daily at an open upstairs window where he would be seen and heard by many.

When Daniel's enemies reported his disobedience to Darius, the king looked for a loophole to excuse Daniel. But Daniel's enemies reminded the king that, by law, the king's decree could not be changed or revoked. So Darius sent Daniel to the lions' den with these words: "May your God, whom you serve continually, rescue you!" (Daniel 6:16). Daniel was sealed up with the lions, and the king spent the night unable to eat or sleep. At dawn, the king went to the lions' den and called to Daniel—and Daniel answered!

"May the king live forever!" Daniel said. "My God sent his angel, and he shut the mouths of the lions" (Daniel 6:21–22). Daniel lived—and the king ordered his rivals to the lions' den. Then King Darius issued a decree glorifying Daniel's God as the one true God.

Daniel's faithfulness to God's truth got him into trouble, bringing him into conflict with the worldly power structures of Babylon. His faith in God's love rescued Daniel and his friends again and again. This is God's model for consistent godly leadership.

"Who shall separate us from the love of Christ? Shall trouble or hardship or persecution or famine or nakedness or danger or sword? As it is written:

'For your sake we face death all day long;
we are considered as sheep to be slaughtered.'

No, in all these things we are more than conquerors through him who loved us." —ROMANS 8:35–37

FOR FURTHER REFLECTION:

1. What are five qualities of godly leadership that you see in the examples of Daniel and his three Hebrew companions?

2. When was a time you felt "targeted" by jealous rivals who made themselves your enemy? What did you do? What do you wish you had done?

3. What expectations do you have of God when you face opposition to your leadership? What expectations do you think God has of you?

4. What steps can you take this week to follow the examples of leadership seen in Daniel and his three companions? Make a list.

25

The Reluctance
of the Queen

Esther 1–4

IN *TABLE TALK*, A COLLECTION OF NOTES FROM MARTIN
Luther's conversations with his students between 1531 and
1544, Luther is quoted as saying he was an "enemy" of the Book
of Esther.[1] He said he wished the book had never been preserved
because it contained "too many heathen unnaturalities." This
statement shows that even a great reformer of the church can be
mistaken about God's Word.

Perhaps one of the "heathen unnaturalities" Luther disliked
is that God is not mentioned by name in Esther. In fact, it is one
of two Old Testament books that do not specifically mention
God (the other is Song of Solomon). Yet the hand of God and
His loving heart are felt throughout both books. Song of Solomon is an allegory of God's love for the Jewish people. And God
is not mentioned in Esther because the Jews in Persia had to be
careful (for political reasons) not to depict the King of Persia as
a mere instrument in God's hand to save the Jews. If you believe

in God, His presence is easily detected in Esther—but His presence would be undetectable to a pagan.

Esther is one of three books in the Bible primarily about women—the Book of Esther, the Book of Ruth, and Song of Solomon. Each is a delightful and engaging love story on the surface—and each contains hidden treasures of meaning just beneath the surface. The Book of Esther has much to teach both men and women about the risks and rewards of leadership.

Again and again in Scripture, God calls a single individual to take a lonely stand for His truth: Moses in Egypt, Daniel in Babylon, Jeremiah in Judah, and now Esther in Persia. In the Book of Esther, we see God call upon a young Jewish woman in a pagan culture during a time of crisis. Her mission is to save the Jewish people from genocide.

To save her people, Esther had to risk everything, including life itself. Though she never mentions the name of God, it's clear that she's a woman of prayer and faith. God is not absent from the story. Invisible? Yes. But absent? No! His actions are on every page and in every line. He is truly the Author of these events.

The story opens with a celebration. King Ahasuerus of Persia held a seven-day feast in his capital city, Susa. After drinking too much, he ordered his queen, Vashti, to appear at the feast and display her beauty. But Queen Vashti refused to be put on display. Enraged, the King deposed and divorced Queen Vashti. Then he had the most beautiful maidens of the kingdom brought before him, and he selected as his new wife a young Jewish woman named Esther (she is one of thousands of Jewish exiles living in Persia). Esther's protector was her cousin Mordecai, an official in the government.

When Mordecai heard of a plot to assassinate the king, he sent warning of the plot through Queen Esther. King Ahasuerus had the conspirators arrested and executed. Mordecai's role in foiling the plot was recorded in the royal chronicles.

When the King's grand vizier, Haman the Agagite, became enraged with Mordecai because the Jewish official refused to bow to him, Haman plotted the death of Mordecai and all the Jewish people. He told King Ahasuerus that the Jews were a troublesome and disloyal people and he offered to pay 10,000 talents of silver to the treasury for a proclamation permitting the extermination of the Jews. The king, not realizing that Esther was Jewish, issued the proclamation.

Hearing the news, Mordecai tore his robes and wore ashes of mourning. He sent a message to Esther in the royal harem, informing her that the King had ordered the extermination of the Jews. He urged Esther to go before King Ahasuerus and plead for her people.

Esther was afraid and reluctant to go before King Ahasuerus. Anyone who approached the King without being summoned could be put to death unless the king extended his golden scepter and let that person live. This law included the Queen. Esther sent word back to Mordecai: she refused to risk death and go before the King.

Queen Esther was afraid—and who can blame her?

Mordecai sent Esther another message: "Do not think that because you are in the king's house you alone of all the Jews will escape. For if you remain silent at this time, relief and deliverance for the Jews will arise from another place, but you and your father's family will perish. And who knows but that you have come to your royal position for such a time as this?" (Esther 4:12–14).

Here is one of those invisible signs of God's presence. Mordecai was confident that his people would be delivered. If Esther refused to help, "deliverance for the Jews will arise from another place." That's a sign of Mordecai's absolute faith in God. When God calls us, we are free to say "no" to Him. But our refusal won't stop God's plan. He has an infinite number of ways to accomplish His will. If we fail Him, He will raise up another— but we will miss out on the honor of serving Him.

Mordecai's reply overcame Esther's reluctance and fear. She sent another message to Mordecai: "Go, gather together all the Jews who are in Susa, and fast for me. Do not eat or drink for three days, night or day. I and my attendants will fast as you do. When this is done, I will go to the king, even though it is against the law. And if I perish, I perish" (Esther 4:16).

So Mordecai carried out Esther's instructions. After three days of fasting, Esther made herself more beautiful than ever and went before the king. What happened next? Stay tuned!

The important thing to see at this point in Queen Esther's leadership journey is that she started out in a state of fear and reluctance. She didn't want to die, so she refused to carry out Mordecai's instructions. Fear is a normal human response to the threat of death.

But for a godly leader, a "normal" response isn't good enough. A leader must face the fear, pray for courage, then act. "Do the thing you fear," said Ralph Waldo Emerson, "and the death of fear is certain."

The key statement in the entire Book of Esther is Esther 4:14, where Mordecai says to her, "And who knows but that you have come to your royal position for such a time as this?" God called Esther out of obscurity and elevated her to the position of Queen of Persia. Why? To save her people at "such a time as this," a time of impending genocide.

When Queen Esther said "yes" to God's call upon her life, she became much more than a mere queen. She became a leader.

"Trust in the LORD with all your heart
and lean not on your own understanding;
in all your ways submit to him,
and he will make your paths straight."

—PROVERBS 3:5–6

"The LORD is my light and my salvation—
whom shall I fear?
The LORD is the stronghold of my life—
of whom shall I be afraid?"

—PSALM 27:1

FOR FURTHER REFLECTION:

1. In your opinion, why is the book of Esther included in the Bible? Defend your answer.

2. If Esther is our example, then you are not a leader by accident. What does that mean for you today? Explain.

3. What gives you courage when you must face a risky leadership challenge? Why?

4. How might you be able to give godly courage to another leader this week? Brainstorm a list of ideas.

26

The Courage
of the Queen

Esther 5

ONCE, WHEN MY WIFE ELAINE AND I WERE GOING THROUGH
a time of intense trial, I received a card of encouragement from a
dear friend who understood the extremes of our pain and emotions. She wrote:

> You may feel helpless right now. The fact is, you *are* help-
> less. There is little you can do but simply persevere through
> these circumstances. I believe God sometimes leads us into
> these places of pain and helplessness to stretch our faith and
> grow our courage.
>
> When we are hurting and unable to change our circum-
> stances, the crutches we always relied on are stripped from
> us, one by one. At that point, God's words and His love
> stand out to us in a way they never could when we had those
> crutches to lean on. We begin to see Him as constant and
> unchanging, and His love becomes irresistible to us.
>
> Finally, Jesus becomes our only alternative. Otherwise,
> death would be the only logical relief.

I believe Esther must have felt she was in a situation like that. She was the Queen of Persia—yet she was helpless. Forces had been set in motion that were bent on the destruction of the Jewish people—*her* people. Her own husband, King Ahasuerus, had signed the death decree that meant genocide for the Jewish population in Persia. She had no option but to trust God and put her life on the line.

Her cousin Mordecai had told her in a message, "If you remain silent at this time, relief and deliverance for the Jews will arise from another place, but you and your father's family will perish. And who knows but that you have come to your royal position for such a time as this?"

She sent her reply to Mordecai: "Go, gather together all the Jews who are in Susa, and fast for me. Do not eat or drink for three days, night or day. I and my attendants will fast as you do. When this is done, I will go to the king, even though it is against the law. And if I perish, I perish."

A short time before, Esther had been reluctant and fearful. But her faith in God had stirred her courage and moved her to action. Though there is no mention of God or prayer in the Book of Esther, we know that, among the Jews, fasting is always linked to prayer, and prayer is always directed to God. So Esther was telling Mordecai to call a prayer meeting. She did not want to go before the king, unsummoned and in violation of Persian law, without three full days of fasting and prayer support.

At the end of three days, she arose to go before the King. There's a remarkable parallel between Esther's actions and the words of Paul to the church in Rome:

> What shall we say, then? Shall we go on sinning so that grace may increase? By no means! We are those who have died to sin; how can we live in it any longer? Or don't you

know that all of us who were baptized into Christ Jesus were baptized into his death? We were therefore buried with him through baptism into death in order that, just as Christ was raised from the dead through the glory of the Father, we too may live a new life. (Romans 6:1–4)

Deliverance begins with the believer's identification with the death of Christ. Though Esther couldn't have understood the symbolic significance of three days of fasting, God knew. Until we truly believe we are crucified with Christ, buried with Him, and raised with Him, we will never understand the deliverance from sin and death He has given us.

The key to the Christian life is living in the knowledge that we are identified with Christ. We have died with Him and we are raised with Him. When you fail, the Holy Spirit will be grieved and He will bring it to your attention so you may repent, be forgiven, and be restored to fellowship with Him.

Esther chapter 5 opens with the words, "On the third day Esther put on her royal robes and stood in the inner court of the palace, in front of the king's hall" (Esther 5:1). The words "On the third day" have a familiar ring—"God raised him from the dead on the third day" (see Acts 10 :40). The third day is the day of resurrection, the day of new life—and that's the day Queen Esther went before the king.

There she stood, the Jewish Queen of Persia, wondering if the king would extend his scepter and receive her—or have her executed for her presumptuousness. She was afraid—and she was incredibly courageous. Courage is not the absence of fear; courage is doing the thing we fear the most, simply because it must be done.

Queen Esther was a trembling mass of courage. Her heart was in her mouth. She knew that King Ahasuerus was subject to unpredictable moods.

But the king didn't notice that his queen was trembling. All he saw was her gentle spirit and her radiant beauty. The Scriptures tell us that he saw Queen Esther standing in the court and "he was pleased with her and held out to her the gold scepter that was in his hand. So Esther approached and touched the tip of the scepter." Then he asked, "What is it, Queen Esther? What is your request? Even up to half the kingdom, it will be given you."

What happened next? More fascinating, suspenseful events than I can go into here. I suggest you read the Book of Esther for yourself. An average reader can read it in less than half an hour, and it has everything a good page-turning novel should have: unforgettable characters, romance, intrigue, suspense, arch-villainy, murder, betrayal, irony, comedy, and action. And the Book of Esther has something else: God's truth, which you can apply to your leadership life beginning today.

The most important lesson we learn from this part of Esther's story is that to be a leader, you must be courageous. Not fearless—every leader experiences fear. But godly leaders face their fears, enlist prayer support from others, spiritually prepare themselves, then courageously do what God has called them to do. You can be courageous even while you're trembling.

Queen Esther said, "If I perish, I perish." Then she carried out her mission. That's the courage of the queen. That's the courage of a godly leader.

"Say to those with fearful hearts, 'Be strong, do not fear; your God will come, he will come with vengeance; with divine retribution he will come to save you.'" —ISAIAH 35:4

"So we say with confidence,
'The Lord is my helper; I will not be afraid.
What can mere mortals do to me?'"

—HEBREWS 13:6

FOR FURTHER REFLECTION:

1. Agree or Disagree: "God is absent from the book of Esther." Defend your answer.

2. What do you do when you're facing a great leadership obstacle and God appears to be silent and/or absent from your situation? Describe it.

3. How are faith and courage interconnected? Explain.

4. What principles of faith and courage do you see in Esther's example that might be applied to the way you lead others this week?

27

The Prayer of
a Godly Leader

Nehemiah 1

I ONCE HEARD A BUSINESS LEADER GIVE HIS TESTIMONY AT
a conference. He said that, in his early Christian life, someone
encouraged him to pray about problems he had in the work-
place, including strained relationships with his boss and fellow
employees.

"I didn't even want to pray for people who were making life
difficult for me," he said. "But I began praying for them, almost
against my will. Soon I saw changes in the way these people
related to me. I think we Christians have an unfair advantage
over those who don't know the Lord! We have instant access to
the One who created the universe. How can those who don't
know God compete with that?"

The Book of Nehemiah reveals the central role of prayer in
the life of an effective, godly leader. In chapter 1, Nehemiah
was in the Persian capital of Susa. He was one among thousands
of Jewish exiles in Babylon, which had been conquered by the
Persian Empire.

Nehemiah was the king's cupbearer, a high position in the Persian royal court. The cupbearer served wine to the king, but was far more than a glorified waiter. The position could only be held by the most loyal and trustworthy member of the king's court. He protected the king from being poisoned, so the king had to be able to trust that his cupbearer could not be bribed. Because Nehemiah was loyal and trustworthy, he was a close adviser to the king.

While serving in this honored position, Nehemiah learned that the city of Jerusalem, the capital of his ancestral homeland, was in ruins. The city walls were broken and the gates were burned. The Jewish homeland lay in ruins and disgrace.

Ruined Jerusalem symbolizes a life that is spiritually devastated. If you are living in defeat and powerlessness, then Jerusalem's desolation is a picture of your life. We devastate our lives with our sins. We make ourselves powerless by giving ourselves over to addictions like alcohol, drugs, gambling, pornography, illicit sex, and so forth. We are devastated and disgraced if a hidden sin is publicly revealed, destroying our reputation.

Or we may feel devastated by sins committed *against* us. Perhaps you were sexually abused as a child or as an adult, and the shame of that abuse has blackmailed you into silence. Or perhaps you've been humiliated by a false attack against your reputation. Or perhaps you are unable to move past the bitterness and pain of a divorce or betrayal.

In Nehemiah, God shows us how to reconstruct our broken lives. The steps Nehemiah took to restore Jerusalem are also the steps for rebuilding a broken human life. Nehemiah shows us that reconstructing a devastated city or a devastated life always begins with prayer. After hearing that Jerusalem lay in ruins, Nehemiah responded: "When I heard these things, I sat down and wept. For some days I mourned and fasted and prayed before the God of heaven" (Nehemiah 1:4).

He responded with an honest prayer, a cry from the depths of his soul. Nehemiah wept, mourned, fasted, and prayed. He poured out the anguish of his soul before God. In this prayer, Nehemiah gives us the pattern for the prayer of a godly leader.

First, he recognized the character of God:

> Then I said: "LORD, the God of heaven, the great and awesome God, who keeps his covenant of love with those who love him and keep his commandments." (Nehemiah 1:5)

Second, Nehemiah confessed and repented of his own sins, the sins of his family, and the sins of his nation:

> "Let your ear be attentive and your eyes open to hear the prayer your servant is praying before you day and night for your servants, the people of Israel. I confess the sins we Israelites, including myself and my father's family, have committed against you. We have acted very wickedly toward you. We have not obeyed the commands, decrees and laws you gave your servant Moses." (Nehemiah 1:6–7)

Nehemiah confronted his guilt and the guilt of his people. There was not a hint of self-righteousness in this prayer. He didn't shift the blame. He recognized that the destruction of Jerusalem and the humiliation of the Jewish people were not random calamities, but the rightful consequences for the sin of the people.

Third, Nehemiah acknowledged God's gracious promises:

> "Remember the instruction you gave your servant Moses, saying, 'If you are unfaithful, I will scatter you among the nations, but if you return to me and obey my commands,

then even if your exiled people are at the farthest horizon, I will gather them from there and bring them to the place I have chosen as a dwelling for my Name.'

"They are your servants and your people, whom you redeemed by your great strength and your mighty hand." (Nehemiah 1:8–10)

Nehemiah reminded himself that God forgives, God redeems, and God mends broken things. If we turn to Him, He will redeem us and bring us home to His dwelling place. He is a God who keeps His word.

Fourth, Nehemiah requested God's help in rebuilding the broken city:

Lord, let your ear be attentive to the prayer of this your servant and to the prayer of your servants who delight in revering your name. Give your servant success today by granting him favor in the presence of this man."

I was cupbearer to the king. (Nehemiah 1:10–11)

Who was "this man" Nehemiah mentioned in his prayer? And what did "this man" have to do with Nehemiah's plan to restore Jerusalem? Nehemiah identified "this man" in the final sentence of chapter 1: "I was cupbearer to the king." Nehemiah was asking God to move in the heart of the King of Persia.

That's a tall order. That's a bold prayer. Nehemiah wanted to approach the king for help in restoring his broken nation—and that would entail great risk. If the king was displeased with Nehemiah's request, Nehemiah could face demotion, imprisonment, or execution. His plan would only work if God arranged the circumstances in Nehemiah's favor.

Where you are rebuilding a broken city, a broken organization, a broken church, a broken family, or a broken life, the place to begin is prayer. The moment we turn to God in prayer, the process of recovery begins.

> *"Also, seek the peace and prosperity of the city to which I have carried you into exile. Pray to the LORD for it, because if it prospers, you too will prosper."* —JEREMIAH 29:7

> *"I urge, then, first of all, that petitions, prayers, intercession and thanksgiving be made for all people—for kings and all those in authority, that we may live peaceful and quiet lives in all godliness and holiness."* —1 TIMOTHY 2:1–2

FOR FURTHER REFLECTION:

1. The ruined city of Jerusalem symbolizes a situation that has been devastated, either by a person's own sins or by the actions of others. What kinds of "ruined cities" are you facing as you try to lead others right now? Describe them.

2. Nehemiah wept, mourned, fasted, and prayed, pouring out the anguish of his soul before God. How do you pour out the anguish of your soul? What helps?

3. What part have you played in creating the hardships you're now facing? What does Nehemiah's example say to you in that regard?

4. As you face hardships that lie ahead, what prayer of faith would you like to pray each day this week?

28

Godly Powers of Persuasion

Nehemiah 2

THE ENGLISH LANGUAGE HAS NUMEROUS SAYINGS AND SLO-
gans urging us to take action when the time is right. In Shake-
speare's *Julius Caesar*, Brutus tells Cassius, "There is a tide in the
affairs of men which, taken at the flood, leads on to fortune"
(Act IV, Scene 3). Brutus is saying that the key to success is acting decisively when events reach high tide. Act too soon or too
late, and your enterprise will be doomed to failure. Seize just the
right moment, and you'll succeed.

In Nehemiah 2, we see Nehemiah waiting and watching for
just the right moment to put his plan into action. He tells us the
exact month and year when his opportunity arrived:

> In the month of Nisan in the twentieth year of King
> Artaxerxes, when wine was brought for him, I took the wine
> and gave it to the king. I had not been sad in his presence
> before, so the king asked me, "Why does your face look so
> sad when you are not ill? This can be nothing but sadness
> of heart."

I was very much afraid, but I said to the king, "May the king live forever! Why should my face not look sad when the city where my ancestors are buried lies in ruins, and its gates have been destroyed by fire?"

The king said to me, "What is it you want?"

Then I prayed to the God of heaven. (Nehemiah 2:1–4)

Nehemiah dates this event as taking place in the month of Nisan of the Hebrew calendar, approximately April on our calendar. His prayer in chapter 1 took place in the month of Kislev, corresponding to our December. From Kislev to Nisan—from December to April—is about four months. Why did Nehemiah wait four months before bringing his problem to the king? During that time, he was often in the king's presence, yet he waited, saying nothing.

Nehemiah doesn't tell us the reason for the delay. But I think it's safe to say that Nehemiah was waiting for the Lord to reveal to him the right time to act. In the month of Nisan, God spoke to Nehemiah, either through the supernatural prompting of God's Spirit or through the arrangement of circumstances—and Nehemiah knew the time had come.

God still works this way in our lives today. He still wants us to wait for His perfect timing, so that He can answer our prayers and arrange events to accomplish His purpose. We are impatient creatures, and we want our prayers answered *now*. We expect God to answer our prayers on *our* timetable, according to *our* expectations.

But God sometimes delays His answers—not because He is cruel or insensitive to our suffering. He delights in giving good gifts to His children. The Scriptures teach us to persevere in prayer until the answer comes.

Nehemiah undoubtedly prayed fervently, daily, with a broken heart. Finally, a day came when Nehemiah presented the cup to the king, and the anguish he felt was etched on his face. The King of Persia asked his servant Nehemiah, "Why does your face look so sad?"

This was Nehemiah's big break, his flood-tide moment, but it was also a crisis point. Nehemiah was in extreme danger. In those days of totalitarian monarchs, the only way to change the government was through assassination. Every time the king took a sip of wine, he bet his life on Nehemiah's trustworthiness. If the king had any reason to doubt the emotional state of his cup-bearer, if the king suspected Nehemiah of being uneasy because he was involved in a murder plot—Nehemiah might lose his head.

So Nehemiah had every reason to be "very much afraid." Yet he knew that God had opened a door of opportunity in response to his prayers.

Nehemiah told the king that the city of his ancestors lay in ruins, and the king asked, "What is it you want?"

Nehemiah responded with what I sometimes call an "arrow prayer"—a quick prayer shot toward heaven as if it were an arrow. In the silence of his thoughts, Nehemiah sent God a plea for help and wisdom.

Then Nehemiah spoke, and it's clear that he had spent a lot of time thinking and praying about what he should say to the king:

> And I answered the king, "If it pleases the king and if your servant has found favor in his sight, let him send me to the city in Judah where my ancestors are buried so that I can rebuild it."
>
> Then the king, with the queen sitting beside him, asked me, "How long will your journey take, and when will you get back?" It pleased the king to send me; so I set a time.

I also said to him, "If it pleases the king, may I have letters to the governors of Trans-Euphrates, so that they will provide me safe-conduct until I arrive in Judah? And may I have a letter to Asaph, keeper of the royal park, so he will give me timber to make beams for the gates of the citadel by the temple and for the city wall and for the residence I will occupy?" And because the gracious hand of my God was on me, the king granted my requests. So I went to the governors of Trans-Euphrates and gave them the king's letters. The king had also sent army officers and cavalry with me. (Nehemiah 2:5–9)

Nehemiah's presentation was tactful and persuasive. Twice he referred to Jerusalem—but not by name. Jerusalem had a reputation as a breeding ground for revolution. So Nehemiah called Jerusalem "the city where my ancestors are buried." He understood that, throughout the Middle East, kings were greatly concerned about their burial. Nehemiah targeted the king's sympathies, presenting a persuasive case. The king was pleased to grant Nehemiah's request.

Leadership involves influence and persuasion. Nehemiah was a godly leader who sought to influence the heart of the king through prayer, wisely chosen words, and honest facts and arguments. His influence was largely built on his sterling character, on the fact that he had built up a stockpile of trust with the King of Persia. Nehemiah is a role model of godly leadership for you and me.

"Do you see someone skilled in their work?
They will serve before kings;
they will not serve before officials of low rank."

—PROVERBS 22:29

"In the same way, let your light shine before others, that they
may see your good deeds and glorify your Father in heaven."

—MATTHEW 5:16

FOR FURTHER REFLECTION:

1. Timing makes a big difference in leadership success or failure. How do you discover when God's timing is ready for you to act? Give examples.

2. Nehemiah was a patient leader, waiting for the right opportunity. On a scale of one to 10, how would you rate your own patience as a leader? Why?

3. Why does God sometimes give us a vision for leadership, then make us wait—weeks, months, even years—before the opportunity to act arrives?

4. What principles of leadership do you see working in Nehemiah that you'd like to imitate tomorrow? Brainstorm a list.

29

Is the Job Big Enough?

Nehemiah 2

I ONCE READ OF A YOUNG MISSIONARY IN CHINA PRIOR TO World War II. He was a recent university graduate just twenty-eight years old, fluent in Mandarin Chinese and a proven leader. An American oil company wanted to open a new operation in China and planned to locate its main office in the city where this young man lived. The oil company officials offered him a job at *ten times* his allowance as a missionary. The oil company executives were shocked when he turned down their offer.

So they came back with a much larger offer. He turned that offer down as well. They came back a third time with an even bigger offer. Again, he declined. Finally, the executives asked him, "What will you take to accept this job?"

"You don't understand," the missionary said. "It's not that the salary is too little. It's that the job is too small."

We are easily lured away from God's will by offers of money, titles, advancement, or other worldly inducements. We tell ourselves, "My motives are godly. I could do so much good if I had more money or a more influential position." So instead of taking on the *big* job God has for us, we accept the small job with the big paycheck. No matter what rationalizations we use, God knows our motives are self-serving, not God-serving. He won't bless the work we do outside His will.

Nehemiah took on the job God called him to—and it was a *big* job: the reconstruction of Jerusalem. With the permission and blessing of the King of Persia, Nehemiah journeyed to Jerusalem. His first task was to size up the job:

> I went to Jerusalem, and after staying there three days I set out during the night with a few others. I had not told anyone what my God had put in my heart to do for Jerusalem. There were no mounts with me except the one I was riding on. (Nehemiah 2:11–12)

He explored the city's broken walls and ruined gates with a few close associates by night. He did not inform the city's priests, nobles, or officials of his plans. Even so, rumors had spread that Nehemiah was planning to help the Jewish people in some way—and those rumors aroused opposition from the enemies of the Jews:

> When Sanballat the Horonite and Tobiah the Ammonite official heard about this, they were very much disturbed that someone had come to promote the welfare of the Israelites. (Nehemiah 2:10)

Sanballat was a devotee of the pagan god Horon, who was worshipped in the land we now call Syria. Sanballat was a Samaritan and an official of the occupation government of the Persian Empire. He probably envied Nehemiah's close relationship with the king.

Tobiah was from Ammon, an ancient nation (corresponding to modern Jordan) that hated the Jews. They worshipped the false gods Milcom and Molech. The Ammonites were descended from Abraham's nephew Lot, so they were related to the Jewish people.

The opposition Nehemiah faced is symbolic of the opposition we face in the Christian life. We grow emotionally and spiritually as we face problems in the power of God. Through times of trouble and testing, God proves to us that we can rely on Him to provide what we need in any situation.

Nehemiah expected to face opposition. He knew it would be a tough job. During his night-time excursions around the city, he measured distances, figured up the building materials he would need, and added up the expenses. Then he factored in the added hindrances and problems that Tobiah and Sanballat would cause. Nehemiah was a realist. He wanted to know exactly what he was getting into.

As we face the brokenness of our own lives, we need to be realists as well. We need to search out the facts and size up the job and take into account the spiritual opposition we face. We do ourselves no favors by denying the truth or shifting the blame. In Alcoholics Anonymous, the first step in healing is admitting the truth to oneself and others: "I am an alcoholic." Until the alcoholic is willing to face that truth, recovery remains out of reach.

Nehemiah personally assessed the challenge before him. Then, once he had taken stock of the problem, it was time to enlist the Jerusalem community in the effort to rebuild the walls:

> Then I said to them, "You see the trouble we are in: Jerusalem lies in ruins, and its gates have been burned with fire. Come, let us rebuild the wall of Jerusalem, and we will no longer be in disgrace." I also told them about the gracious hand of my God on me and what the king had said to me.
>
> They replied, "Let us start rebuilding." So they began this good work. (Nehemiah 2:17–18)

This passage is one of the reasons Nehemiah is regarded as a great role model of godly leadership. Leaders are people who achieve extraordinary results through ordinary people. A challenge this big requires the active involvement of the entire community. It requires a team effort—and every team must have an able, inspiring leader.

Where did Nehemiah study the art of leadership? He undoubtedly learned many crucial leadership lessons as the cupbearer to the King of Persia. He had seen the king struggle with difficult decisions, make plans, and map strategies. He had seen the king take on huge challenges and face violent opposition. Nehemiah had studied under one of the great leaders of the ancient world. He was well-prepared for this moment.

Nehemiah called the people together and told them, in effect, "Look around you. See the ruins of this once-great city. See the trouble we're in. Our nation is disgraced by the fallen condition of our city. Let's work together and rebuild these walls—and let's remove this disgrace from our city and from ourselves."

God had summoned a great leader and had moved the heart of a king. Now it was time for the people of Israel to roll up their sleeves and get to work. Bold, godly leadership usually attracts a following. So it was with Nehemiah. He spoke to the people and he called them to action. They responded enthusiastically, saying, "Let us start rebuilding."

Nehemiah had taken on a job that was big enough for him. He had called a team of people around him to get the job done. Next, he would work shoulder-to-shoulder with them as they rebuilt and restored their broken city and their broken lives.

That's what godly leaders do.

"And let us consider how we may spur one another on toward love and good deeds, not giving up meeting together, as some are in the habit of doing, but encouraging one another—and all the more as you see the Day approaching."

—HEBREWS 10:24–25

FOR FURTHER REFLECTION:

1. What motivated you to take your current leadership role? Is it a job "big enough" for you?

2. What lessons do you learn from the way Nehemiah anticipated opposition? Brainstorm at least three.

3. What does Nehemiah's example say to you about teamwork? Explain.

4. With Nehemiah on your mind, what will your prayers to God sound like this week? Write one by hand.

30

Rebuilding the Walls

Nehemiah 3–6

SIR EDWIN HENRY LANDSEER (1802–1873) WAS AN ENGLISH painter and sculptor, best known for the famous lion sculptures in Trafalgar Square. On one occasion, while traveling in Scotland, he stopped at an inn for food and lodging. During dinner, he overheard a fisherman at the next table telling a story to a friend. The fisherman gestured emphatically as a woman passed his table carrying a pot of tea—and the teapot went flying. Tea splashed on the newly whitewashed wall, leaving an ugly stain.

The innkeeper, of course, was furious at the damage to his wall, but Sir Edwin offered a solution. "I might be able to do something with this stain," he said. He went to his room and retrieved some ink and a brush. Then he proceeded to rework the stain into a drawing of a regal stag. Part of the splashed tea became antlers. The bulk of the stain became the stag's body and legs. The artist added trees and the grass of a meadow. When he had finished, the ugly stain had been transformed into a scene of beauty and majesty.

That's what God wants to do with our lives. He wants to take the ugly stain of sin that has damaged our lives and transform it through His divine artistry into wholeness and beauty.

God achieved this same artistic transformation in the life of the Jews in Jerusalem. He used His servant Nehemiah to restore the broken walls of the city—and to restore the broken lives of His people. God used Nehemiah's leadership to take a mass of defeated, dispirited people and focus them on the task of rebuilding their city. In the process, the people became a community once more.

When we rebuild the broken walls of our lives, we discover the wholeness and beauty that God wants to infuse into us through His infinite creativity. The Book of Nehemiah falls into two divisions. Chapters 1 through 6 cover the *reconstruction of the wall*. Chapters 7 through 13 deal with the *reinstruction of the people*. These are the two parallel themes of Nehemiah—reconstruction and reinstruction.

What does a wall symbolize? The most famous wall in the world is the Great Wall of China. Built over several centuries, it protected the Chinese empire against invasion by the nomadic tribes from the north. The wall stretched along more than 5,000 miles of frontier and was much longer than the United States is wide. Because the walls were extremely thick and high, ancient China rightly considered itself safe from invasion.

The walls of Jerusalem were also walls of protection. After the Babylonian invasion, the walls were torn down, the city lay defenseless, and the Temple was destroyed.

The rebuilding of the city walls symbolizes the reestablishment of the strength of an individual human life. You have probably met people whose defenses have crumbled away. They have become human derelicts, drifting in the streets of our cities, without hope or a future. But God in his grace often steps into the lives of defenseless people and shows them how to rebuild the walls of their lives.

The reconstruction of the walls of Jerusalem are a vivid picture of the way the walls of our lives, the walls of a church, the walls of our communities, and yes, the moral and spiritual walls of a nation can be restored. Just as physical walls provide strength and protection, moral and spiritual walls provide power and purpose for our lives.

Jerusalem is not merely the historic capital of Israel and the center of the life of the nation. Jerusalem is a *tangible symbol* of a human life in which God desires to dwell. The city of Jerusalem is a *picture* of God's chosen dwelling place—but it is not God's *actual* dwelling place. According to the New Testament, *we* are to be the dwelling place of God. Paul wrote, "To them God has chosen to make known among the Gentiles the glorious riches of this mystery, which is Christ in you, the hope of glory" (Colossians 1:27).

That is the destiny God desires for us, that we would be His dwelling place. Jerusalem is the symbol of that relationship, so the picture we see in the book of Nehemiah—a picture of Jerusalem in ruins—is a symbolic representation of a broken human life, a life that has lost its defenses, a life that lies open and vulnerable to wave after wave of terror and destruction.

From time to time, we need to pause, examine ourselves, and see if the walls and gates of our lives are strong. We need to ask ourselves, "Is my life truly God's dwelling place? Or have I allowed the walls of my life to crumble, the gates of my life to fall into disuse and neglect?"

The rebuilding of the walls begins in Nehemiah 3. There we see that all of the people of Jerusalem and the surrounding countryside were involved. They all got sweaty and dirty and everyone worked together. The high priest, Eliashib, and the other priests put their backs into it and rebuilt the Sheep Gate. A high official, Shallum son of Hallohesh, ruler of a half-district of Jerusalem, rebuilt one section with the aid of his daughters. That's right, women rolled up their sleeves and worked alongside the men.

Everyone worked for free. Volunteers streamed in from nearby towns—Jericho, Tekoa, and Mizpah—and from farms and ranches all around. Nehemiah inspired them to work together harmoniously. Twenty times in Nehemiah 3, you see the phrase "next to." Zakkur was rebuilding next to the men of Jericho, Meshullam was working next to Meremoth, and so forth. They motivated and encouraged each other, they built friendships and they cared for each other. Inspired by Nehemiah's leadership, the people worked long hours and achieved far more than they ever thought possible. The result was astonishing:

> So the wall was completed on the twenty-fifth of Elul, in fifty-two days.
>
> When all our enemies heard about this, all the surrounding nations were afraid and lost their self-confidence, because they realized that this work had been done with the help of our God. (Nehemiah 6:15–16)

It was a huge job—and Nehemiah, empowered by God, inspired the people to accomplish months' or years' worth of labor in a mere *fifty-two days*.

In 1983, I accompanied physicist Lambert Dolphin and Israeli archaeologist Nahman Avigad (author of *Discovering Jerusalem*) on a tour through Old Jerusalem. Most of the ancient walls of Jerusalem were destroyed when the Roman General

Titus laid siege to the city in AD 40. Dr. Avigad led us to the top of a section of wall and said, "I have clearly established that this was part of the original wall that Nehemiah built." Words can't express the excitement I felt to be standing at the site where the events in the book of Nehemiah took place. I was standing atop the physical evidence of a leadership miracle, which Nehemiah and his people completed in less than two months.

What big, "impossible" challenge is God calling you to take on for His glory? Who are the people God wants you to assemble into a team of believers, a community of wall-builders? The challenge awaits you. God will provide everything you need for success.

"Like a city whose walls are broken through
is a person who lacks self-control."
—PROVERBS 25:28

"Your people will rebuild the ancient ruins
and will raise up the age-old foundations;
you will be called Repairer of Broken Walls,
Restorer of Streets with Dwellings."
—ISAIAH 58:12

FOR FURTHER REFLECTION:

1. What went through your mind as you read the story of Sir Edwin Henry Landseer and the great tea stain? Why?

2. How does it influence your understanding of your leadership role to realize that you are the dwelling place of God? Be specific.

3. Who stands "next to" you as you undertake the hard work of leading? Explain that relationship.

4. What is the big, "impossible" wall-building challenge you feel God is calling you to take on next? What will you do this week to prepare for that challenge?

31

Leaders Are
Accountable to God

Micah 3

MY MENTOR, DR. H. A. IRONSIDE, TOLD OF AN EXPERIENCE
he had at a restaurant. His meal had just been set before him
when a man walked up to his table and said, "Do you mind if I
sit down with you?"

"Not at all," Dr. Ironside said.

The stranger seated himself across the table and Dr. Ironside
bowed his head and said a silent word of thanks to the Lord.

The man said, "Do you have a headache?"

"No, I feel fine."

"Is something wrong with your food?"

"No. Why do you ask?"

"I saw you with your head down and I thought there must
be something wrong."

"No, I always give thanks to God before I eat."

"Oh," the stranger said, "you're one of *those*, are you? I never
give thanks. I earn my money by the sweat of my brow and I
don't need to thank anybody. I just start right in!"

"Ah," Dr. Ironside said, "you're like my dog. He does that, too."

Human beings who will not give thanks to God are like irrational animals. They lose a bit of their humanity. Even godless people have a duty to worship God. Their unbelief is no excuse, because God's eternal power and divine character can be clearly seen in nature. Paul in Philippians 2:10 tells us that "at the name of Jesus every knee should bow, in heaven and on earth and under the earth"—and those who refuse to willingly bow the knee to Him in this life will bow to Him on the Day of Judgment.

We are all accountable to God, and leaders are doubly accountable. Hebrews 13:17 reminds us that leaders must one day give an account to God for their actions, words, and decisions as leaders. That's the message of the prophet Micah to leaders. Like it or not, we are accountable to God.

The prophet Micah was a contemporary of Isaiah. Like Isaiah, he ministered to the southern kingdom, Judah. Someone has called the book of Micah "Isaiah in shorthand." Micah summarizes many of the predictions and prophecies of Isaiah and even uses some of Isaiah's wording. This is not surprising, since these two prophets labored together.

The key to the Book of Micah is found in the meaning of the prophet's name. In Hebrew, Micah means "Who is like God?" or "Who is like Jehovah?" This is Micah's repeated question throughout the book, and some Bible scholars believe "Micah" was the prophet's nickname, not the name he was given at birth—a nickname based on his oft-repeated refrain of "Who is like God?"

The theme of Micah is *God-like-ness*—a word that has been shortened to "godliness." Godlikeness (or godliness) is also the theme of Paul's epistle to the Ephesians. It's instructive to compare these two messages, Micah and Ephesians, side by side. By doing so, we see that the Old Testament and the New Testament complement each other and speak with a unified, consistent voice.

Micah 1:10–16 contains an interesting use of language that is difficult to appreciate in the English translation. Many ancient prophets enjoyed a good pun, and Micah was one of these punsters. The problem for English-speaking readers is that the puns are in Hebrew. If you could read the original Hebrew, you'd see pun after pun used in the names of cities mentioned by Micah. He tells the city of Gath not to weep —the name of the city means "weeping." He tells Beth Ophrah ("House of Dust") to roll in the dust in repentance. He tells Shaphir ("Beauty") that her beauty will be shamed. He tells Zaanan ("Marching") that it will not march forth. He tells Beth Ezel ("House of Neighbors") it will be left unprotected by its neighbors. He tells Maroth ("Bitter Town") that it will grieve bitterly. He tells Lachish ("Horse Town") to harness the horses and get out of town.

The key section of Micah for leaders is Micah 3, which deals with God's judgment against ungodly (un-God-like) leaders. The ungodly leadership of Judah is the primary reason God is judging the nation.

Do you remember the story about the Greek philosopher, Diogenes? He went around the countryside with a lantern, even in broad daylight. People would ask, "Why are you carrying a lantern in the daytime?" Diogenes would reply, "I'm looking for an honest man."

Like Diogenes, Micah has been tramping around the southern kingdom of Judah, searching for godliness. He looks among the rulers of the nation, but finds only corruption, oppression, bribery, and injustice. Micah declares that the reason for God's judgment upon His people is that those who are authorized to act in God's stead have forgotten that they are responsible to God.

This indictment touches our leadership lives today. God holds all authority accountable to Himself (see Ephesians 6:9). Any leader who forgets that he or she is accountable to God is likely to use power for personal advantage. That's the behavior that corrupted Judah and brought the nation under God's judgment. The prophet writes:

Then I said,

> "Listen, you leaders of Jacob,
> you rulers of Israel.
> Should you not embrace justice,
> you who hate good and love evil;
> who tear the skin from my people
> and the flesh from their bones; . . .
> Hear this, you leaders of Jacob,
> you rulers of Israel,
> who despise justice
> and distort all that is right;
> who build Zion with bloodshed,
> and Jerusalem with wickedness.
> Her leaders judge for a bribe,
> her priests teach for a price,
> and her prophets tell fortunes for money.
> Yet they look for the LORD's support and say,
> "Is not the LORD among us?
> No disaster will come upon us."
> Therefore because of you,
> Zion will be plowed like a field,
> Jerusalem will become a heap of rubble,
> the temple hill a mound overgrown with thickets.
> (Micah 3:1–2, 9–12)

When you serve in a position of authority and leadership—whether in government, in the church, in a business or organization, or in your family—you represent God in that position. When we forget the responsibility we have as leaders, when we forget that we will have to give an account to God for our words, deeds, and decisions as leaders, that's when our leadership turns into corruption, bribery, and oppression. That's when we bring down God's judgment on ourselves.

As leaders, we are accountable to the people we lead, and we are accountable to God. So let's decide now to live the kind of lives we will not be ashamed to give an account for. Let us be leaders who practice godliness—*God-like-ness*—so that we can stand before God and hear Him say, "Well done, good and faithful servant."

"Here is a trustworthy saying: Whoever aspires to be an overseer desires a noble task. Now the overseer is to be above reproach, faithful to his wife, temperate, self-controlled, respectable, hospitable, able to teach, not given to drunkenness, not violent but gentle, not quarrelsome, not a lover of money."

—1 TIMOTHY 3:1–3

FOR FURTHER REFLECTION:

1. In your opinion, how does God judge nations today? Explain.

2. What do you think it means for a leader to be accountable to the Lord today?

3. When have you known a leader that consistently exhibited "God-like-ness"? Describe that person.

4. If you knew that no one but God would see you lead tomorrow, how might that change what you did?

32

The Successful Failure

Mark 14; John 21; Acts 2

IN THE LATE 1800S, A MINISTER NAMED MILTON WRIGHT stood in the pulpit of his church and announced, "You have heard that men are trying to build machines that will enable them to fly like birds. You have also heard that every such attempt has ended in failure. Why? Because men were not meant to fly like birds. These foolish men are trying to do what is contrary to the will of God!"

Bishop Wright was confident, he was emphatic, he was vehement—and he was wrong. In fact, he was proven wrong in 1903 by his two inventive sons, Wilbur and Orville Wright. The more emphatic the prediction, it seems, the more likely it is to be proven wrong—as a disciple named Peter learned to his shame.

On the night before Jesus was crucified, He led the disciples out to the Mount of Olives, and there He told them, "You will all fall away, for it is written: 'I will strike the shepherd, and the sheep will be scattered.' But after I have risen, I will go ahead of you into Galilee."

But Peter emphatically declared, "Even if all fall away, I will not."

Jesus answered, "Truly I tell you, today—yes, tonight—before the rooster crows twice you yourself will disown me three times."

"Even if I have to die with you," Peter insisted, "I will never disown you." Peter was confident, he was emphatic, he was vehement—and he was wrong.

Later that night, in the Garden of Gethsemane, Jesus was arrested and tried before the Sanhedrin. During the trial of Jesus, Peter was in the courtyard near the hall of the Sanhedrin, warming his hands around the fire with the very guards who had arrested Jesus. That was a brave thing to do. Peter placed himself in terrible danger, and I think Peter's pride had brought him that far. He was so determined not to let the Lord down, determined not to deny Jesus.

But then a servant girl of the high priest saw Peter and accused him of being one of the companions of "that Nazarene, Jesus." The accusing words of a mere servant girl caused fear to grip Peter's heart. He answered the girl, saying he didn't know what she was talking about.

The servant girl accused him again, and he again denied knowing Jesus. Then someone else in the courtyard said to Peter, "Surely you are one of them, for you are a Galilean." Peter's accent gave him away. He cursed and swore and said, "I don't know this man you're talking about."

Then the rooster crowed, and Peter remembered what Jesus had told him. Mark's gospel tells us that when Peter heard the rooster crow, "he broke down and wept."

The Greek word translated "broke down" is a very strong term. It literally means that he went out and threw himself on the ground in agony. He wept tears of repentance and remorse. To me, the most hopeful sign in this account is that Peter broke down and wept.

Peter's tears are the tears of failure. But the lesson of Peter's life is that failure does not have to be the end of the story. Peter's tears speak to us of another day, which is recorded for us in John 21.

The resurrected Lord and Peter were together beside the Sea of Galilee. Jesus said to Simon Peter, "Simon son of John, do you love me more than these?" In the past, Peter had often compared himself to the other disciples, saying things like, "Even if all the others leave you, I will not." Jesus seemed to invite Peter to compare himself to the other disciples once more. But Peter was a changed man—changed by failure.

"Yes, Lord," he said, "you know that I love you." This time, he made no boasts, no comparisons.

Jesus said, "Feed my lambs."

A little later, Jesus said again, "Simon son of John, do you love me?"

"Yes, Lord, you know that I love you."

"Take care of my sheep."

Then a third time Jesus said, "Simon son of John, do you love me?"

Peter was wounded by this third question, and he said, "Lord, you know all things; you know that I love you."

Jesus said, "Feed my sheep."

Jesus asked Peter "Do you love me?" three times, once for each of Peter's denials, once for each of Peter's failures. And while asking Peter those questions and commanding him to feed His sheep, Jesus reinstated Peter as a disciple and as a leader.

Jesus chose not to use Peter in a great way until Peter had failed greatly. Throughout the three years that Peter walked with Jesus, he was a proud, boastful, and impetuous man. He continually (and tactlessly) compared himself to the other disciples.

But after this same boastful Peter wept bitter tears of failure, he was finally fit to lead.

God rarely uses anyone in a great way until He has taken that person through failure. Why? Because God can only use us when we've been emptied of pride and are able to empathize with the least and the last and the lost.

Almost immediately after Peter's pride was demolished, God began to use Peter in amazing ways. Peter's dramatic success story began in Acts 2, soon after Jesus ascended into heaven. Peter and the other apostles were in Jerusalem and the Holy Spirit came upon them in a mighty way, with miraculous manifestations.

Then Peter stood up and fearlessly preached the gospel of Jesus Christ to the thousands who were gathered there. It was a powerful salvation message, and Peter closed by saying, "God has made this Jesus, whom you crucified, both Lord and Messiah."

The people who heard Peter's message were convicted of their need for Jesus, and said, "Brothers, what shall we do?"

"Repent and be baptized," Peter said, "every one of you, in the name of Jesus Christ for the forgiveness of your sins. And you will receive the gift of the Holy Spirit. The promise is for you and your children and for all who are far off—for all whom the Lord our God will call."

On that day alone, about 3,000 people received Jesus as their Lord and Savior, and were baptized and added to the church. That's an amazing success story. But Peter's success for Christ didn't take place until after Peter wept tears of brokenness.

"Brothers and sisters, I do not consider myself yet to have taken hold of it. But one thing I do: Forgetting what is behind and straining toward what is ahead, I press on toward the goal to win the prize for which God has called me heavenward in Christ Jesus." —PHILIPPIANS 3:13–14

FOR FURTHER REFLECTION:

1. Think of your biggest failure as a leader. How did that experience change you? Explain.

2. If you were preaching a sermon on failure, using Peter's example as your text, what would be your top three points? Describe them.

3. When someone you lead fails to meet your expectations, what is the best way to confront that failure?

4. When it comes to dealing with failure—yours and others'— what's one thing you'd like to change this week?

33

The Preparation of an Apostle

Mark 14; John 21; Acts 2

WHILE WAITING IN THE HONOLULU AIRPORT FOR AN EARLY morning flight to Tokyo, I bought a newspaper and sat down to read. The first story I read was an account of a young Filipino eye doctor who had come to Honolulu for a medical conference. He was a gifted surgeon who had perfected an operation no one else had done. He demonstrated the procedure to a gathering of fellow surgeons.

I boarded the plane and sat down to await takeoff. A few minutes later, a passenger sat down beside me, a Filipino man. We chatted, and I learned that he was a surgeon. "Oh?" I said. "What sort of surgery do you perform?"

"Eye surgery," he said.

"Ah," I said, holding up the newspaper. "I was just reading about you." I showed him the newspaper story.

He smiled and said, "Yes, that's me."

We talked throughout the flight. He was not a Christian but had recently been thinking about his spiritual condition and wondering if the claims of Christ were true. Before we parted at the Tokyo airport, I gave him a New Testament and told him it was his to keep. We also exchanged addresses.

After concluding my stay in Tokyo, I flew to Manila and visited the eye surgeon at his home. He told me he had been reading the New Testament every day and had invited Jesus Christ into his life as Lord and Savior.

I'm sure God arranged the "coincidence" of placing the newspaper in front of me before I encountered the doctor on the plane. I believe God was preparing this doctor to receive the gospel long before he and I met.

In much the same way, the apostle Paul underwent years of preparation before he became a follower of Christ and a leader in the early church. Prior to his conversion, Paul was known as Saul of Tarsus, a first century Christian's worst nightmare. He threatened and arrested Christians, taking whole families into custody and dragging them off in chains. After his dramatic encounter with the risen Christ on the road to Damascus, Saul was blinded and shaken. He had to be led by the hand until he was healed of his blindness in Damascus.

The Christians in Damascus were afraid to trust Saul. But as time passed, it became clear that Saul's conversion was genuine. Those who had hid from Saul soon embraced him as a brother in Christ. He became their dearest friend and ally.

But before Saul could become a leader in the church, he had to go through a time of preparation and obscurity. He went to Arabia where he studied the Old Testament Scriptures and the Lord Jesus personally instructed him in the truth of the gospel. "The gospel I preached is not of human origin. . . . I received it by revelation from Jesus Christ" (see Galatians 1:11–12).

Instructed by the Messiah Himself, Saul read the Old Testament and found Jesus Christ on every page. He discovered that the Old Testament sacrifices are pictures of the sacrifice of Jesus. The very configuration of the tabernacle is a picture of the life of Jesus. The Lord appears in symbols and pictures throughout the books of Moses, the Prophets, and the Psalms.

As Saul studied and learned, he realized that God had selected him to go to the nation of Israel and show the Hebrew people from their own Scriptures that Jesus was the long-awaited Messiah. Saul probably reasoned, "I'm a Hebrew of the Hebrews, trained as a strict Pharisee, a scholar of the Scriptures from Genesis to Malachi. I have an intense desire to reach my people—so intense that I would wish myself cut off from Christ if it would help me reach my Jewish brothers. Who is better equipped than I to reach my people?"

Saul emerged from the Arabian desert and returned to Damascus, confident he could win his Jewish brothers by proving that Jesus is the Messiah. He went to the synagogues and made his case from the Scriptures. His logic was irrefutable. He won every debate—but he didn't make a single convert. He only succeeded in angering the people he sought to win.

We see the result of Saul's early attempt at evangelism in Acts 9:23–25. His opponents in Damascus conspired to kill him. They watched the city gates, planning to ambush him and murder him when he attempted to leave the city. Saul's friends took him to the city wall by night and lowered him in a basket through an opening in the wall.

From Damascus, Saul went to Jerusalem, where he tried to join the disciples, but they were afraid of him. Finally, Barnabas—whose name means "Son of Encouragement"—took Saul to meet the apostles. Barnabas explained to them that Saul had experienced a dramatic encounter with the risen Lord and had preached the gospel fearlessly in Damascus. Saul stayed for a while in Jerusalem where he again tried to win converts by debating in the synagogues. The result was the same—his opponents plotted to kill him.

During Paul's stay in Jerusalem, he was praying at the Temple when he went into a trance and Jesus spoke to him, saying, "Leave Jerusalem immediately, because the people here will not accept your testimony about me." Saul tried to argue with the Lord, but Jesus said, "Go; I will send you far away to the Gentiles" (see Acts 22:17–21). Jesus was saying, in effect, "You're not running your life any longer. I am. I have something entirely new and different planned for you. Don't argue with me. Obey me. That's the only way I can work through you. Until you learn that, you will never be of any use to me at all."

So Saul stopped arguing and started obeying. At the Lord's insistence, Saul reluctantly left Jerusalem and headed home to Tarsus. He stayed there at least seven years and perhaps as long as ten years. During that time, Saul learned gentleness and humility.

As a young Christian, a new convert, Saul was filled with an intense love for Jesus, but he also possessed all the zeal of the flesh. He desperately wanted to do God's work—but he wanted to do it in his own argumentative way. He wanted to win converts to Christ, but all he did was stir up trouble. Many immature Christians are like that—full of zeal but lacking humility.

Jesus said, "Take my yoke upon you and learn from me, *for I am gentle and humble in heart*, and you will find rest for your souls" (Matthew 11:29, emphasis added). Immature Christians need to temper their zeal with gentleness and humility. If we have zeal like Saul but lack the humility of Christ, we only get in the way of the gospel.

Saul disappears from the Book of Acts from the latter part of chapter 9 until almost the end of chapter 11. When Saul returns, he is accompanied by Barnabas. Saul is a changed man—humbled, chastened, and obedient to God. He will soon become known as the mighty apostle Paul.

What is the difference between the new Paul and the old Saul? The new Paul is easy to recognize because he wears the yoke of Christ upon his neck.

"Wisdom's instruction is to fear the LORD, and humility comes before honor."
—PROVERBS 15:33

"Humble yourselves, therefore, under God's mighty hand, that he may lift you up in due time."   —1 PETER 5:6–7

FOR FURTHER REFLECTION:

1. How did you meet Jesus? Describe what happened.

2. How does your first meeting with Jesus continue to influence the way you lead others today? Be specific.

3. What part does humility play in effective leadership and mentoring? Make a list of at least five things.

4. Jesus said, "Take my yoke upon you and learn from me." What realistic steps can you take this week to do that?

34

Preparing the Young Leader

---

1 Timothy; 2 Timothy; Titus

I ONCE DELIVERED THE COMMENCEMENT SPEECH AT BIG Sky Bible College, about forty miles from the little Montana town where I grew up. I arrived a day early and took a sentimental journey to my old hometown. I saw many of my old high school classmates and was amazed to find the town was pretty much as I remembered it.

The most nostalgic experience of the trip was driving past the acreage, about a mile out of town, where a rancher and his wife once lived. I had spent several years working there as a ranch hand. The couple had practically adopted me as a son while I was in high school.

My own father, a railroad man, had abandoned my mother and me when I was small. Because I grew up without a father, this rancher became a stand-in father to me. He mentored me, encouraged me, and instilled in me the virtues of manhood. All those memories came flooding back as I visited the place where I spent many happy hours.

The apostle Paul wrote three letters to young leaders—two letters to Timothy and one to Titus. In all three letters, Paul stirs up warm memories like those I had of that Montana rancher, my stand-in father. Paul wrote, "To Timothy my true son in the faith," "To Timothy, my dear son," "To Titus, my true son in our common faith."

Paul met Titus during his lengthy stay with Barnabas in Antioch of Syria, following his first missionary journey. There Paul led Titus to Christ. He discipled Titus, and this young Gentile Christian became Paul's right-hand man, secretary, interpreter, and fellow missionary. And Paul met Timothy during his second missionary journey, when he and Silas visited Timothy's hometown of Lystra.

To Paul, Timothy and Titus were sons, and these three letters reveal the fatherly love and pride Paul felt for them. Paul traveled with Timothy and Titus around the Roman Empire and designated them as his representatives to the churches. He left Titus on the island of Crete to lead the church there. He took Timothy to Ephesus and placed him in charge of the church there.

The book of Acts closes with Paul under house arrest in Rome, preaching and teaching in a rented house. Various early accounts suggest that Paul was later released and he went to Macedonia, then west to Spain. Paul probably wrote the letters of 1 Timothy and Titus during these travels. After Spain, Paul probably revisited Greece and Asia Minor (modern Turkey). Scholars believe he was arrested in Troas, taken to Rome, and imprisoned in the dungeon of Rome's Mamertine Prison, where he wrote 2 Timothy. It was not long after that, tradition tells us, that Paul was beheaded on the Ostian Way, outside of Rome.

Much of Paul's teaching in these three letters is focused on mentoring—both his mentoring of his sons in the faith, and their mentoring of others. Paul understood the importance of mentoring in his own walk with Christ.

Paul's first mentor in the Christian faith was Ananias of Damascus. When God told Ananias in a vision to seek out Saul of Tarsus, lay hands on him, and give him back his sight, Ananias was afraid. He knew Saul's reputation as a persecutor of the church. But God said, "Go! This man is my chosen instrument to proclaim my name to the Gentiles and their kings and to the people of Israel" (Acts 9:15). Ananias could hardly have imagined that Saul of Tarsus would become a great missionary, the apostle Paul.

As a young Christian, Saul was also mentored by Barnabas (see Acts 11), who taught him the value of a gentle and humble spirit.

Timothy faced difficult challenges in Ephesus, a major Mediterranean seaport that was also a hotbed of pagan goddess worship and immorality. Paul's letters to Timothy suggest that this young pastor faced pressures and crises in his ministry. The people of Ephesus looked down on him because of his age. So Paul wrote, "Don't let anyone look down on you because you are young, but set an example for the believers in speech, in conduct, in love, in faith and in purity" (1 Timothy 4:12).

Paul knew the moral dangers Timothy faced in Ephesus. He counseled Timothy to maintain a standard of purity in his speech and conduct. Purity is the platform from which an effective ministry proceeds. Without a pure life, Timothy's gospel would mean nothing.

The apostle reminded Timothy that the Word of God is central to an effective ministry. "Devote yourself to the public reading of Scripture, to preaching and to teaching," Paul wrote, adding, "Watch your life and doctrine closely. Persevere in them, because if you do, you will save both yourself and your hearers" (see 1 Timothy 4:13,16). The Word must be the hub of everything that takes place in the life of the church.

Paul knew that strong-willed people in the church took advantage of Timothy's gentle, easygoing demeanor, so he wrote, "For the Spirit God gave us does not make us timid, but gives us power, love and self-discipline" (2 Timothy 1:7). Paul gave Timothy practical guidance on how to lead the church through difficult circumstances.

The apostle gave similar instructions to Titus. He encouraged Titus to teach the older men "to be temperate, worthy of respect, self-controlled, and sound in faith, in love and in endurance." He should teach older women "to be reverent in the way they live, not to be slanderers or addicted to much wine, but to teach what is good. Then they can urge the younger women to love their husbands and children, to be self-controlled and pure, to be busy at home, to be kind, and to be subject to their husbands, so that no one will malign the word of God." He urged Titus to teach the young men "to be self-controlled" (see Titus 2:2–6).

It's significant, I think, that Paul told Titus to teach the older women, and that the older women should teach and mentor the younger women. But Titus himself should mentor the younger men. Paul was aware of the temptations that might arise if he were to teach the young women himself.

Paul knew that young men could be prone to coarse jesting and unsound speech. Titus needed to be a role model: "In everything set them an example by doing what is good. In your teaching show integrity, seriousness and soundness of speech that cannot be condemned, so that those who oppose you may be ashamed because they have nothing bad to say about us" (Titus 2:7–8).

These three letters contain penetrating insights regarding God's plan for the healthy functioning of His church. Many churches and church leaders have wandered from these principles, with tragic results. If we will study these letters and apply their truths to our leadership lives, we will become the wise and godly leaders our Lord intended us to be.

> *"Then our sons in their youth*
> *will be like well-nurtured plants,*
> *and our daughters will be like pillars*
> *carved to adorn a palace."*
> —PSALM 144:12

> *"Not many of you should become teachers, my fellow believers, because you know that we who teach will be judged more strictly."*
> —JAMES 3:1

FOR FURTHER REFLECTION:

1. Who has played the role of a spiritual father or mother in your life? What are the most important principles you learned from that person?

2. What parallels do you see between the culture where Timothy lived in Ephesus and the culture that surrounds you today? How does that affect the way you lead?

3. If Paul were writing you a letter today about the leadership role you play, what do you think he'd advise?

4. Paul encouraged his "sons" in the faith to "set an example for the believers in speech, in conduct, in love, in faith and in purity." What can you do tomorrow to pursue that charge?

35

The Gifted Leader

---

1 Timothy 1:18–19; 2 Timothy 1:6

DURING A BREAK FROM MY STUDIES AT DALLAS THEOLOGI-cal Seminary, I worked as a summer youth minister at a church in Pasadena, California. At that time, Dr. Lewis Sperry Chafer, the president and founder of Dallas Theological Seminary, came to Pasadena for a speaking engagement. He graciously spent an afternoon with my wife Elaine and me.

I took Dr. Chafer to the church where I worked and showed him around the impressive buildings. The congregation at that time did not have a pastor, though they were seeking one. Dr. Chafer said, "Ray, do you think you might end up here, pastoring this church?"

"Who knows what God will do? I don't have any particular plans."

"It would be a good place for you. I believe God is going to give you a great ministry."

I don't know what he had in mind when he said that, but his words were a great encouragement to me. Many times over the years, especially during times of trial and difficulty, I've recalled Dr. Chafer's words and drawn hope from the bright future he envisioned for me. I think I have a sense of how Timothy must have felt when he read these words from his spiritual mentor, the apostle Paul:

> Timothy, my son, I am giving you this command in keeping with the prophecies once made about you, so that by recalling them you may fight the battle well, holding on to faith and a good conscience, which some have rejected and so have suffered shipwreck with regard to the faith. (1 Timothy 1:18–19)

Often, the biggest difference a leader can make in a young leader's life is to see that person's potential and say, "I see great things ahead of you. God can use your life in a big way." That was a role Paul played in the life of this young leader named Timothy.

Paul first met Timothy during his second missionary journey, when he and Silas visited the city of Lystra in Asia Minor (modern Turkey). Timothy had a Jewish Christian mother and a Greek father. Acts 16:2 tells us that the Christians of Lystra and Iconium spoke well of Timothy, so Paul enlisted him as a companion on their missionary journey. Paul became Timothy's mentor, and Timothy shared Paul's hardships and sufferings on the missionary road, while being trained by the greatest missionary of all time.

At some time in Timothy's early life—perhaps after his conversion and profession of faith—the elders of the church in Lystra laid hands on Timothy, and one or more of them made prophetic utterances over him, stating that Timothy would be used in a great way by God. So in his letter to Timothy, Paul reminds him of the words the elders spoke over him.

The elders at Lystra had envisioned great things ahead of young Timothy, and Paul did as well. That prophecy of

Timothy's future was an encouragement and a motivator for this young leader. Paul reminds Timothy of that prophetic word, and he says, in effect, "Timothy, you are my son in the faith. As a son wants to please his father, I know you want to please your spiritual father. So I am writing these instructions to encourage you to fulfill the great future that was envisioned for you."

Years ago, a young man said something that struck me very forcibly. His father, whom he had idolized, had just died. So this young man said to me, "What do you do when the only man you ever wanted to please is dead?" I sensed that this young man had lost his motivation to accomplish great things. We all want to live our lives to please someone, and when that is taken from us, we lose a big piece of our reason for living. I encouraged him to live to bring honor to his late father's memory—and that suggestion seemed to help him.

Timothy wanted to please his spiritual father, the apostle Paul. He was undoubtedly encouraged by Paul's fatherly words.

Later, near the end of Paul's life, he wrote a second letter to Timothy. He opened that letter with a similar reminder of a time early in Timothy's life when Paul himself laid hands on Timothy and confirmed a spiritual gift in him. Paul wrote: "For this reason I remind you to fan into flame the gift of God, which is in you through the laying on of my hands" (2 Timothy 1:6).

Spiritual gifts are more than mere talents or skills. A spiritual gift is an endowment or power or grace given by the Holy Spirit which enables Christians to fulfill the mission of the church. Few Christians have their spiritual gifts affirmed by a laying-on of hands, as Timothy did, but every Christian has spiritual gifts.

The Scriptures list at least twenty-one different spiritual gifts: apostle, prophet, evangelist, pastor, teacher, service, exhortation, giving, leadership, mercy, helps, administration, wisdom, knowledge, discernment, prophecy, tongues, interpretation, faith, healing, and miracles. You'll find the gifts listed in Romans 12:3–8, 1 Corinthians 12:1–12, 27–30, and Ephesians 4:11.

Paul is saying to Timothy, in effect, "You have received a spiritual gift. Make sure you put it to good use." Bible scholars have debated which of the gifts Paul was referring to. Some think it was the gift of evangelism because, in Paul's second letter to Timothy, he writes: "Do the work of an evangelist, discharge all the duties of your ministry" (see 2 Timothy 4:5). But we really don't know which gift Paul was referring to.

Timothy undoubtedly had the gift of a pastor-teacher, and other gifts besides. The Holy Spirit generally gives clusters of gifts to His people, not just one gift. Every human being is a kaleidoscope of gifts, and God uses all these facets and hues of supernatural ability to convey His love and truth to the world. Timothy was certainly aware of his gifts, and he knew what Paul meant when Paul urged him to put his gift to good use.

As godly leaders, let's heed the words of the apostle Paul. Let's discover our spiritual gifts and fan them into flame. And let's heed the example of Paul, who mentored young leaders like Timothy and encouraged them to discover and use their gifts. That's how the Lord Jesus builds His church, as we use our gifts, serving one another, teaching and preaching His truth, each generation mentoring the next, from age to age to age.

"As iron sharpens iron, so one person sharpens another."
—PROVERBS 27:17

"Follow my example, as I follow the example of Christ."
—1 CORINTHIANS 11:1

FOR FURTHER REFLECTION:

1. Who was the first person, other than a family member, to tell you that you could have a future as a leader? How did that influence you?

2. What would you say is your strongest spiritual gift? How are you using that gift today?

3. In what ways could you encourage someone else in the use of his or her spiritual gifts? Brainstorm a list of at least five ideas.

4. Paul told Timothy to "fan into flame the gift of God, which is in you." If you were to follow that advice each day this week, what would that look like? Be specific.

36

Fight the Good Fight

---

1 Timothy 1:18–19

AUTHOR AND PASTOR CRAIG BRIAN LARSON SUGGESTS AN analogy between the Christian life and the life of the Alaskan bull moose. Every fall, the bulls in the moose herd battle each other for dominance, using their antlers as weapons. If a bull moose's antlers are broken in battle, he must surrender. The moose with the strongest antlers triumphs.

Though the battles are fought in the fall, they are won or lost in the summertime when the moose nourishes himself. The moose who consumes the most complete diet for gaining muscle and growing sturdy antlers will prevail in the fall.

There's a lesson for us all. Our enemy, Satan, will attack us at a time and season of his choosing. Will we be victorious? Or will our spiritual "antlers" be broken and the battle lost? The battle is decided not in the time of warfare, but in the time of preparation. Are we nourishing ourselves for battle? Are we gaining spiritual muscle and strengthening our spiritual antlers for the clash ahead? Victory depends how we prepare ourselves *today*.

That is Paul's over-arching theme in 1 Timothy, his letter to a young leader he has been mentoring. He expresses that theme early in the letter when he tells Timothy he is writing so that "you may fight the battle well, holding on to faith and a good conscience" (1 Timothy 1:18–19). Paul wants Timothy to know that the Christian life is warfare, and he doesn't want Timothy to face that battle unprepared.

Paul writes in definite terms. He doesn't say, "Fight *a* battle well." He says, "Fight *the* battle well." The Christian life is the *only* battle worth fighting. It is not *a* fight; it is *the* fight. What is the object of spiritual warfare? Is it to survive until the end of life? Is it to be the last soldier standing? No. Sometimes success in battle demands a sacrifice, including the ultimate sacrifice, death itself.

The list of Christian martyrs who have given their lives fighting this good fight could fill countless books, beginning with the first martyr, Stephen, whose execution by stoning was witnessed and approved of by Saul of Tarsus, the future apostle Paul. All of the apostles (with the possible exception of John) suffered violent martyrdom.

In more recent times, A Polish Franciscan friar, Maximilian Kolbe, voluntarily died in place of a stranger at Auschwitz in 1941. Dietrich Bonhoeffer, leader of the Confessing Church in Germany, was hanged by the Nazis at Flossenbürg in 1945. Nate Saint, Jim Elliot, Pete Fleming, Ed McCully, and Roger Youderian were martyred with spears while taking the gospel to the Auca people of Ecuador in 1956. Christian pastor Wang Zhiming was executed during the Chinese Cultural Revolution of Chairman Mao in 1973. Janani Luwum of the Church of Uganda was murdered by forces of Ugandan dictator Idi Amin in 1977.

I could go on—but the important question is this: All these Christians who died serving Christ—did they die in vain? No. They died fighting the good fight. They died fighting the spiritual battle. Even in death, they are victors and conquerors in spiritual warfare.

During World War II, on D-Day, June 6, 1944, the Allied landing craft approached the beaches of Normandy and the doors came down so that the soldiers could wade ashore. Many soldiers were killed by German machine gun fire before they could even step out of the landing craft. Were their lives wasted? No. The bullets their bodies absorbed would have killed the men behind them if they had not stood in the line of fire. Their deaths were tragic, yet they shared in the victory of battle. They died—but they died as conquerors. Even in death, they helped liberate Europe from Nazi oppression.

Christians wage the good warfare, they fight the good fight, and they sometimes fall in battle. Those who fight the good fight are walking in the footsteps of Jesus. He went before us, fighting the battle we now fight. He lived on the battlefields of this life. He went out into the marketplaces, the city streets, the temple courts, and he braved the dangers there. He went out into the midst of life and He subjected himself to opposition and persecution. He was our great example of what it means to wage the good warfare of the Christian life.

Spiritual warfare is redemptive, compassionate warfare. People are not the enemy, even people who hate us and oppose us. As Paul wrote, "For our struggle is not against flesh and blood, but against the rulers, against the authorities, against the powers of this dark world and against the spiritual forces of evil in the heavenly realms" (Ephesians 6:12).

Who is our enemy? Satan and his demons. The moment we start to battle other people, whether Christians or non-Christians, we have stopped fighting the good fight. People are not our enemy. People are *victims* of the true enemy. Some are brainwashed by the enemy, some are hostages of the enemy, some do the bidding of the enemy, but they are not our enemy.

How do we fight the good fight? Paul says we must hold fast to two things: *faith* and a *good conscience.*

Faith is believing what God has told you. Faith is believing the truth about God's sovereign control of history and His love for Adam's lost race. Faith is believing in the cross of Christ and the blood of Christ and the resurrection of Christ. Faith enables us to face the uncertainties and perils of the future with confidence in God. We can fight the good fight and wage the good warfare, knowing that no matter what happens to any individual soldier, the battle has already been won. So we hold on to this faith and we do not lose heart.

And with faith there must also be a good conscience. Our conscience wasn't given to teach us the difference between right and wrong. The purpose of the conscience is to *help us to act according to the truth of God's Word.* We need a conscience to help us to *choose* what is right and *resist* what is wrong.

A good conscience is the armor that protects your soul. Satan cannot discourage the spiritual warrior whose faith is strong, nor wound the warrior whose conscience is clean. A good conscience is synonymous with an obedient heart, a heart that wants to do what God says is right.

Whenever you are about to make a choice between what God says and what your feelings tell you, obey God. Do that and you'll maintain a good conscience. You'll be a spiritual "bull moose," well prepared to fight the good fight.

"No weapon forged against you will prevail,
and you will refute every tongue that accuses you.
This is the heritage of the servants of the LORD,
and this is their vindication from me,"
declares the LORD. —ISAIAH 54:17

"Be alert and of sober mind. Your enemy the devil prowls
around like a roaring lion looking for someone to devour. Resist
him, standing firm in the faith, because you know that the
family of believers throughout the world is undergoing the same
kind of sufferings." —1 PETER 5:8–9

FOR FURTHER REFLECTION:

1. In what ways do you see the Christian life, and Christian leadership, as a spiritual battle?

2. The examples of Christian martyrs remind us that sometimes people die in spiritual battle. What does that reality mean to you? Describe it.

3. What would you say are the top five "best practices" when facing a spiritual battle?

4. "A good conscience is the armor that protects your soul." How might remembering that statement influence the way you approach your leadership role this week?

37

The Lord's Leaders

1 Timothy 3

WHEN I WAS IN SEMINARY, I SPENT TWO SUMMERS AS AN intern with radio Bible teacher Dr. J. Vernon McGee. After seminary, I spent three months traveling with Dr. Harry A. Ironside, the longtime pastor of Moody Memorial Church in Chicago. I was privileged to be mentored by these two legendary Bible teachers.

Dr. Ironside committed his life to Christ as a child. He taught adult and children's Sunday school classes when he was eleven years old. As a teenager, Harry Ironside was known as "The Boy Preacher," delivering more than 500 sermons a year with the Salvation Army. In 1929, he became senior pastor of Moody Memorial Church in Chicago.

By 1950, suffering from cataracts in both eyes, he was nearly blind. For three months in 1950, I was his chauffeur, secretary, and companion. I had just graduated from Dallas Theological Seminary and he became my mentor in the ministry. I took dictation for him, and he'd sometimes add a short note in a large script, reminding me of Paul's words, "See what large letters I use as I write to you with my own hand!" (Galatians 6:11). He impacted my life in unforgettable ways.

Soon after he and I parted, I was called to serve as the first pastor of a two-year-old fellowship in Palo Alto, California, which later became Peninsula Bible Church. At age thirty-two, I was the pastor of people who were older and wiser than I. Some were nationally known Christian leaders. I felt inadequate and often wished I could talk to Dr. McGee or Dr. Ironside and draw upon their wisdom and experience.

I eventually spent nearly four decades as pastor of Peninsula Bible Church, retiring in 1990. As my hair turned white and my face grew lined with age, I encountered many newly minted pastors, fresh out of seminary. They asked me the same questions I used to ask my mentors and they reminded me of my younger self—and of a young pastor named Timothy.

I'm sure Timothy often longed to talk to Paul as he faced problem after problem in Ephesus. He must have been overjoyed to receive the letter we now know as 1 Timothy—a letter rich in leadership insights. One key chapter is 1 Timothy 3, Paul's instructions on the qualifications for leaders in the church. He writes: "Here is a trustworthy saying: Whoever aspires to be an overseer desires a noble task" (1 Timothy 3:1).

The role of an overseer or elder was not invented by human beings. It was ordained by Jesus, the Head of the church. When Jesus, after His resurrection, sent the disciples out as apostles, He instructed them to lay the foundation of the church. That foundation was the apostolic teaching concerning the work and person of Jesus. Who were the leaders of the first local church body, the Jerusalem church? The apostles—the disciples Jesus trained and mentored for three years.

Jesus designated the kind of leaders who would lead His church, and He determined how those leaders should function in the church. Unfortunately, too many churches today are run like corporations. Decisions are made by a board of directors according to the business practices of the world. That's not the Lord's model for the church.

The church was born out of the death and resurrection of Jesus Christ. The first mark of a true church is that it shares the life of Christ. Every true member of His church is born of the Spirit and filled with the Spirit. The church is not like any other human organization.

In 1 Timothy 3, Paul gives us guidelines for the kind of people who should serve as elders or leaders in the church. First he gives us a list of character traits that should mark an elder's life. Then he lists the accomplishments that should be part of an elder's spiritual résumé. Let's examine the character qualities Paul lists:

> Now the overseer is to be above reproach, faithful to his wife, temperate, self-controlled, respectable, hospitable, able to teach, not given to drunkenness, not violent but gentle, not quarrelsome, not a lover of money. (1 Timothy 3:2–3)

To be above reproach is to demonstrate a desire to live a righteous life. An elder isn't perfect, but if he sins, he admits it and corrects it. To be faithful to one's wife (literally, a "one-woman man") means that he must keep his marriage vows. To be temperate is to have a serious-minded demeanor; he must not be given to uncontrolled outbursts of emotion. He must be self-controlled; his behavior must be guided by the Holy Spirit.

He must be respectable—that is, dignified and orderly. He must be hospitable—the kind of person whose home is open to friends and strangers alike. Like the Good Samaritan, he helps strangers in time of need. An elder must be able to expound the

Scriptures, recognize error, and correct those who misuse God's Word.

An elder must not be "given to drunkenness." Wine was commonly consumed by Christians and pagans alike. Paul does not say that elders should not drink wine, but that they should not drink to intoxication. Also, an elder must not be violent but gentle. He must not be an angry, contentious man who causes dissension. He must have a gentle spirit.

He must not be quarrelsome. In the original language, the word translated "quarrelsome" conveys a sense of being stubborn and insisting on one's own way. Finally, an elder must not be greedy. He must be generous, selfless, and focused on serving, not on being served.

Next, Paul describes the record of accomplishments an elder should have:

> He must manage his own family well and see that his children obey him, and he must do so in a manner worthy of full respect. (If anyone does not know how to manage his own family, how can he take care of God's church?) He must not be a recent convert, or he may become conceited and fall under the same judgment as the devil. He must also have a good reputation with outsiders, so that he will not fall into disgrace and into the devil's trap. (1 Timothy 3:4–7)

The first accomplishment to look for is a well-managed family. His children should be obedient and respectful. The word *children* suggests small children in the original language. Paul recognizes that, in adolescence or the teen years, a child from a good Christian home may go astray due to peer pressure and other influences.

A recent convert is also disqualified. Becoming mature in Christ takes time. Many newly converted Christians are joyful and enthusiastic about their faith. They easily share Christ with others. They are earnest and sincere, but spiritually immature. They lack the wisdom that comes from experience. There's the risk that a position of leadership could make the recent convert proud and conceited—and pride is the sin by which Satan fell.

Finally, an elder must have a good reputation with outsiders. In my early years as a pastor, I spoke with the pharmacist at a store near our church. I mentioned a man who attended our church, and the pharmacist frowned and said, "Don't mention his name around here."

I was shocked. "Why do you say that?"

"He may attend your church, but I know him better than you do. He's owed me money for six months and has never paid a dime."

The church member was respected by everyone—except this pharmacist. I decided to suspend judgment but avoided placing too much responsibility on him for a while. A few weeks later, I learned that this man had been leading an immoral life. It's easy to put on a "Sunday face" and fool other church members, but the people who see you Monday through Saturday see the real you.

Those who qualify and accept the responsibilities of an elder have chosen a noble task. Pray for your leaders. Support them and learn from them. They have been ordained by the Lord Himself to serve the body of Christ.

"Keep watch over yourselves and all the flock of which the Holy Spirit has made you overseers. Be shepherds of the church of God, which he bought with his own blood." —ACTS 20:28

"To the elders among you, I appeal as a fellow elder and a witness of Christ's sufferings who also will share in the glory to be revealed: Be shepherds of God's flock that is under your care, watching over them—not because you must, but because you are willing, as God wants you to be; not pursuing dishonest gain, but eager to serve; not lording it over those entrusted to you, but being examples to the flock. And when the Chief Shepherd appears, you will receive the crown of glory that will never fade away." —1 PETER 5:1–4

FOR FURTHER REFLECTION:

1. Look at Paul's list of qualifications for a church leader in 1 Timothy 3:2–5. What stands out to you in this list? Why?

2. If you had to rank, in order of importance for your specific leadership position, the items from 1 Timothy 3:2–5, what would your list of qualifications look like? Explain your rankings.

3. What obstacles keep someone from living up to the qualifications listed in 1 Timothy 3:2–5? What helps that person?

4. As you examine these qualifications for leadership, what changes would you like to make in your leadership or mentoring efforts? How can you begin making those changes tomorrow?

38

A Leader, Not a Boss

1 Corinthians 4:1–2

A YOUNG PASTOR SAID TO ME, "TELL ME WHAT YOU'D DO IF you were in my shoes. The board of elders at our church called me in and said, 'You need to understand that you're employed as pastor, but this is our church, not yours. We were here before you came, and we'll be here after you leave. So you to take orders from us. If you don't agree, your days as pastor here are numbered.' How would you respond to such an ultimatum?"

I said, "I would call the elders together and say, 'Brothers, I've thought about what you said. I see two serious theological errors in your position. First, this is not your church. This is the Lord's church. In Matthew 16:18, Jesus said, "On this rock I will build *My* church." We are all servants under His authority. Second, you think you hired me as an employee, but I didn't come here on that basis. I'm a servant, not an employee. I'm grateful to receive financial support so I can devote my full time to the ministry of the Word. But I'm your partner in ministry, according to the New Testament, not your employee. If you don't accept those terms, I'll turn in my resignation.'"

This young pastor went to his elders, said exactly what I

suggested—and the board fired him. A few months later, he told me he was ministering at another church that shared his view of the ministry.

Many churches treat their pastors as "employees." The job description for these "employees" includes preaching, teaching, counseling, performing weddings and funerals, conducting meetings, managing the staff, mentoring interns, visiting the sick and shut-ins, refereeing disputes, writing a newsletter column, and unjamming the office copier.

But the notion of a pastor as a "professional Christian" was unknown in the New Testament church. A minister of Jesus Christ in the New Testament was anyone—literally *anyone*—who, by virtue of the gifts of the Spirit, was qualified to preach and teach the Word of God. In the New Testament, a church does not have one "minister," the pastor. As believers, we are *all* ministers of Christ, we are *all* servants in His church, we are *all* to be ready at *all* times to minister in His name.

A healthy church will have many "ministers"—Sunday school teachers, Bible study leaders, youth volunteers, and people who regularly share the gospel with friends and neighbors over a cup of coffee. That's why we have all been given spiritual gifts to exercise in the church and in the world around us. Paul writes:

> This, then, is how you ought to regard us: as servants of Christ and as those entrusted with the mysteries God has revealed. Now it is required that those who have been given a trust must prove faithful. (1 Corinthians 4:1–2)

The original Greek word for "servants" in this passage is *huperetes*, which literally means "under-rowers." Everyone in Corinth understood what that word meant. Corinth was a major port city where the war galleys of the Roman Empire often docked. The Corinthians knew that the lowest deck of a Roman war galley was comprised of rows of benches. The rowers sat on those benches and powered the ship. The captain stood on a raised platform in the bow, and the rowers were required to instantly obey the captain's orders. These were the *huperetes*, the under-rowers, the servants of the master of the ship. They lived, worked, and died at his bidding.

The under-rowers of the church are servants, without status or rights. They live and die at Christ's bidding.

In all too many churches today, people misunderstand the biblical model for authority and leadership in the church. Too many Christians think a church should have a boss who sets the agenda and gives the orders. They think people need permission from the boss before making a decision and carrying out ministry. The Bible doesn't support such a view.

Christians should never need permission to exercise their spiritual gifts. They should never have to ask the pastor if it's okay to teach a home Bible study or minister to the needs of children in the neighborhood. The pastor's job is to encourage, motivate, and liberate people to exercise their gifts—not hinder them.

When a congregation thinks rightly about its leaders, rivalries and jealousies are sharply reduced. I have seen many churches split because a rivalry has developed between two leaders in the church. Half the church lines up behind one leader and half behind the other—and the church comes apart like a cracked walnut.

Conflict often arises because a minister thinks too highly of himself. By "minister," I don't necessarily mean a member of the so-called "clergy," because a minister can also be a layperson with ministry gifts. God gave us spiritual gifts to empower us to carry out the ministry of the church—*not* to give us a reason for boasting. We can't take credit for the gifts of the Spirit. We can only thank God, in all humility, that He chooses to use us for *His* glory.

A young minister preached to his congregation, and God richly blessed his sermon. Many accepted Christ or rededicated their lives to Him. Later, the young minister strode through the front door of his home, gave his wife a big hug, and said, "Honey, I wonder how many really great preachers there are in the world!"

"One less than you think," she tartly replied.

As the apostle Peter reminds us, we must clothe ourselves with humility because "God opposes the proud but shows favor to the humble" (1 Peter 5:5). When we become proud of the gifts we have received from God, we set the stage for conflict in the church. We are tempted to disdain others whose gifts are different from ours. Let's use our ministry gifts and leadership gifts wisely and humbly, remembering that all the glory belongs to the Giver, not to us.

"He has shown you, O mortal, what is good.
And what does the LORD require of you?
To act justly and to love mercy
and to walk humbly with your God."
—MICAH 6:8

"As a prisoner for the Lord, then, I urge you to live a life
worthy of the calling you have received. Be completely humble
and gentle; be patient, bearing with one another in love. Make
every effort to keep the unity of the Spirit through the bond of
peace." —EPHESIANS 4:1–3

FOR FURTHER REFLECTION:

1. In your current leadership role, what does it mean for you to be an "under-rower" of Christ? Explain.

2. How does an "under-rower" of Christ empower people to use their own gifts and initiative freely? Be specific.

3. A Christian leader is called to lead by serving—how does that work in your situation?

4. What are five principles of leadership that you see in 1 Corinthians 4:1–2? How will you enact those principles this week?

39

The Radical,
Creative Holy Spirit

Isaiah 43:19; 2 Corinthians 5:17

MY FRIEND RON RITCHIE SERVED ON THE PASTORAL STAFF of Peninsula Bible Church and later founded an evangelism ministry called Free at Last. After he joined our staff, he told me of an incident at the Walnut Creek Presbyterian Church, where he had previously served.

The pastors had noticed a great number of new Christians joining the church, all from one part of town. Upon investigating, they discovered that one member of the church worked as a milkman in that area of the town. While going on his route, he got to know his customers and would talk to them about Jesus. Over time, he won many of his customers to Christ, and they began coming to church.

When the leaders of the church discovered the impact this milkman was having for Christ, they went to him and said, "We can see that you have the gift of an evangelist. We want to identify with you and stand with you in prayer. When you go out and witness, our prayers will go with you. If there is anything you need, we will help you."

So they gathered around this man as he knelt, and they all laid hands on him, prayed for him, and commissioned this milkman-evangelist.

The church is the key to society and to life. If the church is not functioning as it should, society will be dysfunctional. Society has become increasingly sick because the life of the body of Christ has ceased to flow.

We are seeing a dramatic rise in violence, depravity, pornography, crimes against children, political corruption, and incivility in society *because the church is not being salt and light in our society*. The church is not being the church. The church has too little influence on the world because the world has too much influence on the church.

The only hope for the world is the church of Jesus Christ. The life of the church, dispersed into the world through its members, is the only hope for healing the social structures and power structures of our world. It's the only hope for healing neighborhoods and promoting brotherhood throughout our world.

If we are not truly loving one another and using our spiritual gifts in the church and in the world, then we are not having an impact on our world as God intended us to. God is calling us to listen to His Spirit and allow Him to lead us in radically new and creative avenues of ministry. He is calling us to realize that there are no limits to what an infinite God can do through Christians who are completely open to His leading.

A number of years ago, a San Francisco-based Christian group wanted to do something about the sex-oriented nightspots in the city's infamous North Beach area. So they organized nightly protests in front of The Condor Club and other striptease clubs. Each night, about a dozen Christians would carry signs and walk the sidewalk in front of the clubs. Protesting is one of the most highly protected activities in San Francisco, so there was nothing the clubs could do to stop the protesters.

As a result of the Christian protests, attendance at the clubs declined sharply. The manager of one of the clubs finally had enough, and he sent a bouncer out to intimidate the Christians and order them to leave. The Christians, knowing they had a legal right to be on the sidewalk, stayed put. The bouncer confronted them several nights in a row—and the Christians responded respectfully but firmly refused to go. Finally, the bouncer got so angry that he punched one of the Christians in the mouth.

Clearly, these protests were risky—but the Christians wouldn't back down. When they arrived the next night, the bouncer again ordered them to leave. "We'll go on one condition," the leader of the Christian group said. "Just let us go inside and pray for all the people there."

The club manager agreed—anything to get rid of those Christians! So the group filed into the club and went up on the stage where a number of scantily-clad dancers stood. The band went silent. The patrons sat slack-jawed at their tables. The Christians took the microphone and prayed for the manager, the bouncer, the young women on the stage, and the customers at the tables. They asked God to reveal His truth to these people and show them their need of a Savior.

As the Christians prayed, the bouncer closed the doors so the street noise wouldn't disturb the prayer meeting. The patrons and performers bowed their heads as they were being prayed for. The place was as quiet as a church. When it was over, there was no mocking or sneering, just a respectful silence as the Christians filed out.

That is the radical creativity of the Holy Spirit. Radicalism is an inclination to use new methods to bring about revolutionary change in society. Without question, the Holy Spirit's methods are revolutionary. No church evangelism committee could ever dream up an idea as radical as a prayer meeting in a striptease club.

Unplanned, impromptu events like that only happen when the creative Holy Spirit moves unhindered through our lives. When the Spirit moves, we should never say, "That's never been done before!" When the Spirit moves, things change. When the Spirit moves, we must follow.

As God said through the prophet Isaiah, "See, I am doing a new thing! Now it springs up; do you not perceive it? I am making a way in the wilderness and streams in the wasteland" (Isaiah 43:19). And Paul reminds us that God make makes all things new: "Therefore, if anyone is in Christ, the new creation has come: The old has gone, the new is here!" (2 Corinthians 5:17).

God's sovereignty and creativity work hand-in-hand with human activity, as God's people make themselves available to Him. If we will listen to the voice of His Spirit, we will see lives changed and our culture renewed as God's truth goes out in surprising, radical, creative new ways.

"So he said to me, 'This is the word of the LORD to Zerubbabel: "Not by might nor by power, but by my Spirit," says the LORD Almighty.'" —ZECHARIAH 4:6

"For it will not be you speaking, but the Spirit of your Father speaking through you." —MATTHEW 10:20

FOR FURTHER REFLECTION:

1. When was the last time you deliberately "commissioned" someone as a means of recognizing and supporting that person's giftedness? Why doesn't that happen more often in the church?

2. How are you using your spiritual gifts—both inside and outside the church?

3. God, speaking in Isaiah 43:19, says, "See, I am doing a new thing." What's one "new thing" you'd love for God to do? What's one "new thing" you've noticed God doing?

4. What is one thing you can do each day this week to help you, as a leader, become more open and sensitive to the creativity and ingenuity of the Holy Spirit?

40

One Generation Away

---

2 Timothy 2:1–2

DAWSON TROTMAN FOUNDED THE NAVIGATORS, AN INTERnational evangelism and discipling organization, when he was in his late twenties. For more than two decades, the Navigators flourished under his leadership.

On the night of June 17, 1956, when Dawson was in his early fifties, he and his wife Lila were driving on a country road in the Adirondack Mountains of New York. Daws abruptly pulled the car to the side of the road and said, "Lila, would you take some notes for me? I believe the Lord is going to call me home soon. There are some things the Navs ought to do during the next five years if I'm not around."

So Lila took notes as her husband dictated. When he was satisfied that she had gotten it all down, he pulled the car back onto the road and proceeded on his way.

The next day, June 18, Dawson was boating with friends on Schroon Lake during a break from a Navigators conference. He was at the controls of a speedboat. The water was choppy but not dangerously so. As he cruised around the lake, the boat bumped over the wake of another boat. The jolt tossed two girls overboard.

Daws knew that one of the girls couldn't swim. He pulled the boat around and shut off the engine. A strong and confident swimmer, Daws dove into the water.

He swam to the first girl and got her into the boat. Then he swam to the second girl and brought her back. She climbed into the boat without trouble.

Someone said, "Where's Daws?"

He had a reputation as a joker and a strong swimmer. Someone said, "He swam under the boat. He'll come up on the other side." But he didn't come up. In fact, his body would not be found for three days.

Soon after the accident, one of Daws' friends broke the news to Mrs. Trotman. "Oh, Lila," he said, weeping, "I'm so sorry. Dawson's gone!"

Lila took the news calmly, quoting Psalm 115:3: "Our God is in heaven; he does whatever pleases him." Lila Trotman saw her husband's death as a controlled event, the timing of which was determined by God's sovereign will.

God had given Dawson Trotman a sense that his time was short, and that inkling enabled him to prepare his organization to continue without him. Daws poured his life into the people he led, and though they grieved, they carried on the work of the Navigators.

When the apostle Paul was in Mamertine Prison, knowing that the time of his departure was approaching, he wrote to his spiritual son Timothy, "You then, my son, be strong in the grace that is in Christ Jesus. And the things you have heard me say in the presence of many witnesses entrust to reliable people who will also be qualified to teach others" (2 Timothy 2:1–2).

Leader, are you entrusting God's truth to reliable people—to your congregation, your children, your employees, your interns, your students, your neighbors? Are you entrusting God's truth to the people you lead, to people who are qualified to teach others? Are the things you have learned rippling out into the world in expanding circles of influence and blessing?

God, through Paul, is speaking to Christians everywhere. God expects all believers to be communicators of His truth. He has given each of us as Christians this precious deposit of His truth, and he expects us to transmit this truth to the next generation.

Whether you are a preacher or teacher, a stockbroker or stocking clerk, a corporate CEO or a stay-at-home mom, be a leader and a communicator of God's truth. Mentor and disciple others by both word and example. Pour your life into faithful people and entrust this deposit of truth to their care.

Timothy must have seen Paul in times of discouragement and times of rejoicing. Through it all, Timothy had seen the blessings of the gospel spread throughout the world. He had seen lives changed and communities transformed. So Paul reminded Timothy of all he had seen and heard in his travels with the beloved apostle: "The things you have heard me . . . entrust to reliable people."

How do you know if a person is reliable and faithful? Let me suggest to you four qualities I always look for when I seek to mentor and disciple someone:

First, I look for a person with a teachable mind, someone who is ready and willing to learn. I look for people who are hungry for truth and serious about following Jesus Christ.

Second, I look for a person with a humble heart, someone who is more concerned for God and others than for building his own reputation.

Third, I look for a person with an identifiable spiritual gift. Paul mentions this qualification when he says to entrust these truths to reliable people who are "qualified to teach others." He is speaking of the spiritual gift of teaching. Spiritual gifts enable Christians to minister, so that the gospel will spread from person to person, and the church will grow.

Fourth, I look for a faithful spirit. I look for a person who has demonstrated a willingness to keep going when the going gets tough. I look for someone who is reliable, dependable, and loyal—someone who can be counted on to keep commitments.

A searching mind, a humble heart, an evident gift, a faithful spirit: When you find a Christian with these qualifications, pour your knowledge, faith, wisdom, and experience into that person. Mentor that person, just as Jesus mentored the Twelve, just as Paul mentored Timothy and Titus.

Every church is just one generation away from apostasy. The work of a church can fall apart in a single generation if the leaders fail to transmit God's truth to the next generation. Faith is not absorbed by osmosis. It must be faithfully taught, by parents to children, by leaders to followers, by mentors to disciples. Those who are old and wise in the faith must entrust their wisdom to the young.

No leader lives forever, but great leaders live on in the lives they influence. Jesus knew He was going to die, and He prepared His disciples to carry on after His death and resurrection. Paul knew he was going to die, and he prepared Timothy to carry on. Dawson Trotman knew he was going to die, and he prepared the Navigators to continue on.

Leader, you are called to entrust God's truth to reliable people. They will entrust it to other reliable people. And those people will entrust it to others, on and on, generation by generation, one soul after another, until the Lord returns.

> *"He decreed statutes for Jacob*
> *and established the law in Israel,*
> *which he commanded our ancestors*
> *to teach their children,*
> *so the next generation would know them,*
> *even the children yet to be born,*
> *and they in turn would tell their children."*
> —PSALM 78:5–6

FOR FURTHER REFLECTION:

1. What strikes you most about Dawson Trotman's life and death? Explain.

2. What would you say are the top five ways to entrust God's truth to reliable people—to your congregation, your children, your employees, your interns, your students, your neighbors? Brainstorm a list.

3. "A searching mind, a humble heart, an evident gift, a faithful spirit." In what ways does that statement describe you? How does it describe those you lead or mentor?

4. Now that you've reached the end of this book, what will change in the way you think about leadership? And what will you do differently from here on out? Write yourself a letter to answer those questions.

AFTERWORD

A Letter from Jim Denney

"LEADERS," RAY STEDMAN SAID, "ARE PEOPLE WHO ACHIEVE extraordinary results through ordinary people." The Bible is filled with examples of such leaders, the ordinary people they led, and the extraordinary works God did through them:

- Jesus, the Twelve, and the founding of the church.
- Gideon, his three hundred warriors, and the victory over the Midianites.
- Nehemiah, the people of Jerusalem, and the rebuilding of the walls.
- Paul, the missionaries he mentored, and the expansion of the early church.

Ray Stedman preached and lived the biblical model of leadership. He was a faithful expositor of the Scriptures and a leader of character and integrity. He was open-hearted, loving, and humble. He understood that a leader is not a boss but a servant.

As I edited this book, I was privileged to spend many hours reading Ray's other books—*Body Life, Adventuring through the Bible, God's Unfinished Book, Psalms: Folk Songs of Faith,* and more. From them, I distilled his most practical and penetrating leadership wisdom into these pages. As I have been living in the truths of this book these past few months, I've noticed that the history of Israel and the history of the early church were shaped by leaders who were chosen and anointed by God.

When Ray preached his first sermon at Peninsula Bible Church, he preached about the role of leadership in the church under the New Covenant. His sermon was not recorded and Ray's notes for that message have been lost, but his wife Elaine recalled that his text was Ephesians 4:11–13:

> So Christ himself gave the apostles, the prophets, the evangelists, the pastors and teachers, to equip his people for works of service, so that the body of Christ may be built up until we all reach unity in the faith and in the knowledge of the Son of God and become mature, attaining to the whole measure of the fullness of Christ.

Pastor Stedman saw the church as a living organism—a body, not an institution. The Lord intended that all the members of His church should manifest the life of the body. Under the Old Covenant, there was a clear division between the priesthood and the laity. But under the New Covenant, the leaders of the church—those who had spiritual gifts of an apostle, a prophet, an evangelist, a pastor, or a teacher—were responsible to equip the Lord's people for works of service. The leaders were to instruct, encourage, and train the people to use their spiritual gifts in service to God and others. There's no division between clergy and laity. Every member is a minister.

What is the ministry God calls all believers, all members of the body, to carry out? We are to share our faith with our neighbors and coworkers. We are to serve the needy and outcast. We are to visit the sick, the widows, the orphans, the shut-ins, the prisoners. We are to welcome strangers. All of us in the body, without exception, are ministers to each other and to this broken world.

When we live out the truth of Ephesians 4, a miracle takes place in the church, the body of Christ. Ray called this miracle "body life."

Early in his ministry at Peninsula Bible Church, Ray realized that relationships in the church were shallow and superficial. Everyone wore a Sunday smile and pretended to be problem-free. So Ray and the elders prayed for a breakthrough. They encouraged the people to become more honest about their problems, but to no avail.

Then during an evening "sharing service," after several people had asked for prayer for some minor problems in their lives, one woman stood and said, "My husband and I are here because we need prayer. We haven't spoken to each other all week."

A startled hush fell over the gathering.

"Thank you for sharing that," Ray said. "How many couples here tonight have had a similar struggle in your marriage?"

A hundred hands went up around the room.

The woman gasped and said, "I thought we were the only ones with this problem."

Moments later, someone stood and prayed for this woman and her husband, and for others who struggled in their marriage relationships.

Ray later pointed to that night as the beginning of a new era of transparency and caring in the congregation. Finally, people dropped their pious façades and admitted their flaws and hurts to each other. They discovered they could be open and vulnerable, and their brothers and sisters in the body would love them and pray for them.

The change that began that night radiated out into the

community. The congregation of Peninsula Bible Church became known as a community of people who loved, accepted, welcomed, and cared.

Soon hippies and street people started showing up on Sunday mornings, packing the pews and jamming the aisles. Young people with love beads, tie-dyed shirts, and bare feet were embraced by men in tailored suits and women in their Sunday finery. The word spread far and wide: If you needed help, if you needed the love and grace of Christ in your life, you could find it at PBC.

Ray Stedman preached and lived out a Christlike balance of grace and truth. He loved and accepted people right where they were, even in their helplessness and sin. He didn't say, "You change, you get cleaned up, then you can come to our church." He said, "You're welcome here. You're loved here. We don't condone sin, but we accept sinners, and we won't condemn you."

It was a privilege and a joy to spend so many hours in the words and thoughts of this godly leader, and to select some of his practical and biblical insights on leadership. I have been changed by the hours I've spent inside the mind and heart of Ray Stedman. As you carry the wisdom of Ray's serving heart into your leadership role and mentoring relationships, I'm sure you'll be changed as well.

Notes

Chapter 1
1. James Allan Francis, *One Solitary Life*, Bartleby.com, Number 916, http://www.bartleby.com/73/916.html.

Chapter 3
1. Martin H. Manser, editor, *The Westminster Collection of Christian Quotations* (Louisville, KY: Westminster John Knox Press, 2001), 299.

Chapter 8
1. W. Somerset Maugham, "The Verger," collected by Jaya Sasikumar and Paul Gunashekar, editors, *Spectrum: An Anthology of Short Stories* (Kolkata, India: Orient Longman, 1977), 82–91; some dialogue condensed and adapted.

Chapter 18
1. Marc Fisher, "Clinton's Pastor with a Past," *Washington Post*, September 28, 1998, http://www.washingtonpost.com/wp-srv/style/daily/clinpastor0928.htm.

2. Gordon MacDonald, *Rebuilding Your Broken World* (Nashville: Thomas Nelson, 2003), 185.

Chapter 20
1. Woodrow Wilson, "The Bible and the Soldier," *Selected Addresses and Public Papers of Woodrow Wilson*, edited by Albert Bushnell Hart (New York: Modern Library, 1918), 217–218.

Chapter 25

1. William Hazlitt, translator and editor, *The Table Talk of Martin Luther* (London: H. G. Bohn, 1857), 11.

Enjoy this book? Help us get the word out!

Share a link to the book or
mention it on social media

Write a review on your blog, on a retailer site,
or on our website (dhp.org)

Pick up another copy to share with someone

Recommend this book for your
church, book club, or small group

Follow Discovery House on
social media and join the discussion

Contact us to share your thoughts:

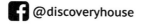 @discoveryhouse    @DiscoveryHouse

Discovery House
P.O. Box 3566
Grand Rapids, MI 49501 USA

Phone: 1-800-653-8333
Email: books@dhp.org
Web: dhp.org